Simple Steps to SMART SUCCESS

Simple Steps to SMART SUCCESS

Laureen Reynolds

Crystal Springs
SDE BOOKS

a division of Staff Development for Educators

Peterborough, New Hampshire

Published by Crystal Springs Books
A division of Staff Development for Educators (SDE)
10 Sharon Road, PO Box 500
Peterborough, NH 03458
1-800-321-0401
www.SDE.com/crystalsprings

Published 2013
Printed in the United States of America
17 16 15 14 13   1 2 3 4 5
ISBN: 978-1-935502-62-3
e-book ISBN: 978-1-935502-63-0

The contents of this book have been published with the permission of
SMART Technologies ULC (www.smarttech.com). SMART Board®, SMART
Notebook®, SMART Exchange™, and the SMART® logo are trademarks of
SMART Technologies ULC and may be registered in the European Union,
Canada, the United States and other countries.

Contents

Contents

Contents

A Wizard's Guide to SMART Tools and Techniques

SMART Exchange: exchange.smarttech.com

More Online Options

Introduction

I started using a SMART Board® more than 15 years ago. Since then, the SMART Board has come a long way—and so have I. When I first saw a SMART Board (it was parked in the computer lab at my school), I had never heard of this device, and I certainly didn't know how to use it. No one else in my school knew how either. So one day, out of curiosity, I signed it out.

Just moving the board to my classroom was a bit of an ordeal. I rolled it down the hallway and wrestled it into the freight elevator, fitting it in on the diagonal, but stranding myself behind it. With some moderate contortions, I managed to press the *down* button. Arriving on the first floor, I pushed and prodded the screen out of the elevator and wheeled it into my classroom. Then I wrangled with cords, projectors, and computers. The rodeo continued as I figured out how to operate the board's buttons and pens and how to connect to the Internet. (Was there even any software for it back then?) But finally, after sacrificing many lunchtimes and planning periods, I put together a four-page lesson about polar animals that included links to pictures and websites. It was truly a miracle.

My initial experience with a SMART Board was especially miraculous because I am not the first person to rush out to buy the latest gadget or newest phone. I am *not* a pioneer when it comes to tweeting, posting, friending, or blogging. I'm not a techie—I'm a teacher. I am passionate about good teaching, and I am willing to experiment with anything that has the potential to enhance the learning experience for students. I know in my heart that, when used purposefully, technology will serve our students well. In fact, it's a great opportunity to engage and motivate students. So if you've been hesitant about integrating your SMART Board into your classroom, I encourage you to dig in and start figuring out how to make it work in your favor. That's exactly why I decided to write this book—to serve as your friend and guide.

Let's get started!

A Day in the Life of a SMART Board

In my work as a consultant, I am continually amazed and delighted to witness all the ways that teachers use a SMART Board in their classrooms. You can teach your SMART Board to do many things, and you can keep it busy all day long. Let's take a quick tour of the possibilities:

✓ As students enter the classroom, they stop in at the SMART Board to move their name to the *Present* category and to indicate their lunch preference.

✓ Each morning, you and your students gather to read and complete the Morning Message displayed on the board.

✓ At calendar time, you use your SMART Board to display the weather, rename the date, and review how many days of the school year have transpired using base-ten blocks.

✓ Prior to an independent writing activity, you ask your students to help you complete a piece of interactive writing at the SMART Board that mimics what they'll then be working on individually.

✓ Word problems are on tap for math. You and your students use virtual manipulatives to solve math problems.

✓ At center time, while you work with small groups, some students stop by the SMART Board to try their hand at a self-checking word sort.

✓ There's a new story in your reading series: You display some pictures from the story and ask your students to predict how the story will turn out.

✓ Each day you practice spelling words in a new way at the SMART Board. Today, you and your students find them in a word-search activity. Tomorrow, you might use the *Screen Shade* tool to play a spelling word reveal game with your students.

✓ For a science unit about animal habits and habitats, you link to an online "zoocam" so that your students can observe a baby panda and record their observations in their science journals.

✓ It's time to board the buses, but before your students leave, they earn their "exit ticket" by responding to a question at the SMART Board about the day's math lesson.

Wow! Who knew your SMART Board could do so many things?

You're Getting SMARTer

Are you feeling a little overwhelmed by possibilities? That's natural. Learning anything new can be challenging, intimidating, maybe even scary, and learning how to use your SMART Board and SMART Notebook® software is no different. This book can act as your SSS—SMART Support System. My goal is to save you the stress and lost time that result from poking around aimlessly at a computer keyboard.

I've created a SMART chart to help you figure out where you are in the continuum of SMART Board users. Take a look at the chart, and think about which description fits you best. If you're a Nervous Novice, that's no cause for alarm. Everyone starts out there, but the good news is that you'll quickly find yourself moving to the Vanna White and Working SMARTer levels. And you'll have fun as you grow in confidence and skill! Each and every new tool, technique, or creative instructional strategy you try on your SMART Board takes you one step closer to being truly comfortable with it—even those experiments that don't work out the way you thought or wanted. I've designed this book to help you along the pathway to becoming a Totally SMART SMART Board user, no matter what point you start at.

SMART Chart

Read through the descriptions below, and note the ones that fit you best right now. You may discover that you're in between levels, and that's okay. Revisit this chart as you work with the activities in the book, and note your progress.

> No matter where you start, you can take simple steps to SMART success!

	Nervous Novice	Vanna White	Working SMARTer	Totally SMART
Teacher Interaction with SMART Board	I use it as a projection screen.	I move objects on the SMART Board while my students watch.	I have my students operate the board under my supervision.	I design lessons that include student use of the board without my direct supervision.
Teacher Use of SMART Tools	I wonder what all those tools in the toolbar do.	I experiment with using tools in the toolbar.	I have customized my toolbar.	I feel comfortable showing others how tools work.
Teacher Use of SMART Notebook Software	I only make use of pages created by others.	I feel comfortable customizing an interactive template.	I'm eager to create original pages from scratch.	I'm ready to design multilayered, multipage lessons.
Management of Student Interaction with SMART Board	I don't ask my students to interact with the board.	I sometimes ask a student to work at the board while others watch.	I engage my class in conversations while work is happening at the board.	I extend interactivity to students not at the board by using manipulatives.
Frequency of Use	I use my board once a week or less.	I use my board once or twice each day for a specific task.	I use my board in more than one subject area, more than one time each day.	I use my board during direct instruction in every subject and also for assessment and clerical tasks.

Interaction = Achievement

On the SMART chart on page 3, you may notice the emphasis on interaction both at the board and in the "audience" as you make your way to becoming Totally SMART. As you use the SMART Board more and more in your classroom, your skill at increasing interactivity with the board will grow. It will become a natural part of your planning process, and that's so important. A study by Marzano and Haystead (2009) shows that the more students interact with the SMART Board throughout the school day, the higher student achievement gains are. The same study also shows that it takes up to two years for a teacher to become proficient in using the board—so don't feel discouraged if you have some frustrations and failures early on. Strive to use your board as often as possible each school day. Not only will your students become more proficient, but so will you. Then you'll want to use it even more. Your progress will escalate, and so will your confidence!

Think of a time recently when you were using your SMART Board or watching someone else use one. For how many students was the board actually interactive at any given time? Chances are—one. Yup, just one out of 20, 25, or even 30 students. That needs to change. I have even developed a mantra about it: *When possible, in some way, shape, or form, whatever is happening at the board needs to be happening in the "audience" as well.* In other words, if one student is interacting with the board to show the date using virtual coins, then students

In *Brain-Based Teaching in the Digital Age* (2010), Marilee Sprenger points out that interactive whiteboards help today's students—whom she calls "digital natives"—connect with information in the way that is most familiar to them: on a screen. She reminds us that not only can students view information on this giant screen but they can also manipulate, annotate, and communicate it, alone, in pairs, and during whole-group instruction.

who are sitting on the floor or at their desks should have actual coins to work with too. If a student at the board is writing labels using a *Pen* tool, students not at the board should have a cut-and-paste version to work with.

Sometimes interactivity takes place in the form of conversation with you while the child at the board is thinking or working. That's fine; just be sure to plan the topics of conversation in advance. For example, if the student at the board is labeling a picture with adjectives, you might ask students *not* at the board to tell you some other adjectives they know or to name an adjective that describes a particular part of the picture displayed on the board.

Occasionally, there is no natural way to have everyone interacting, and the best approach is to focus the group's attention solely on the SMART Board. That's okay too, as long as it is the exception and not the rule.

Since keeping each activity interactive for all of your students is paramount, there are suggestions for increasing interactivity throughout this book. Whole-group involvement may take the form of a game, a group response using props, or the use of manipulatives and conversation while one student is interacting with the board. As you master SMART Notebook tools and become more experienced with the SMART Board, you'll naturally pass along basic board skills to all of your students.

SMART Boards Don't Teach; Teachers Do

A final thought before you dive in: Good teaching is still good teaching. The versatility of a SMART Board is amazing, but it is only one tool on your tool belt of good teaching practices. You still need to strive for variety in your instructional approach and offer multiple pathways for learners to help them reach the learning goal. Your students need opportunities to engage in conversation with each other and to be active. Throughout the school day, challenge them to problem-solve, work together, and practice the skills and concepts you've taught them. Look for ways your students can work in a variety of groups with a variety of peers on a variety of tasks.

A SMART Board doesn't have mystical powers. It cannot create engaging lesson plans and projects. It cannot bring a passion for learning to your students. It can't even turn itself on. It needs you to bring it to life, just as you bring to life your students' learning experiences. YOU are still the creator of the magic in your classroom.

A SMART Board doesn't have mystical powers. YOU are still the creator of the magic in your classroom!

How to Use This Book

I've designed this book to start with the very basics of using the SMART Board in the classroom. Each turn of the page adds another layer of instruction and helpful tips. Even if you have very little previous experience with a SMART Board or SMART Notebook software, you can be successful with the ready-to-use activities presented in Section 1—and all of the SMART Notebook files for these activities are available for you to download from the Internet. Section 2 focuses on the use of SMART Notebook interactive templates, which are designed to be flexible and easy to work with. Each one has a distinctive fun, interactive element, and I've provided clear instructions for accessing and adapting these templates. (The activity pages themselves are available to you online too!) If you like creating computer-based activities with unique content that's designed especially for your students' needs and activities, you'll love the sample activities and in-depth instructions for building customized pages in Section 3.

To help you get the most out of every activity in this book, I've created voice-over demonstrations to coach you in leading each activity. You can access these demonstrations using the Web link address provided for each activity. For activities in Section 2, I've also created demonstrations of how to work with the interactive templates; for Section 3, there are demonstrations of how to build each activity page from scratch.

No matter where you dip in you'll find great things to learn and explore at the turn of every page. Plus, I've created online demonstrations!

SECTION 1:
Follow Along with Ready-to-Use Pages

Start here to learn the basics of working with a SMART Board and the software.

Lead activities using ready-to-use pages.

Build confidence and encourage the habit of frequent use.

SECTION 2:
Get On Board with Interactive Templates

Begin to interact with SMART Notebook software.

Lead activities created using SMART Notebook interactive templates; learn how to modify the templates yourself.

Gradually increase your competence with the software.

The activities in this book are designed to do three things:

1 To inspire and instruct you in the use of your SMART Board during every part of your instructional day

2 To engage and motivate your students through the integration of technology and interactivity

3 To help you develop your skills so that you can take your SMART Board use as far as you want to go

Section 4 is both a quick-reference guide and an introduction to the wider world of SMART Notebook online. A Wizard's Guide to SMART Tools and Techniques is the place to turn whenever you need a fast explanation or refresher about how to use a particular SMART Notebook tool, tab, or menu function mentioned in the book. Following the Wizard's Guide, you'll find information about SMART Exchange™. I'll tell you where to look on this website to see how other educators are using the SMART Board and to discover even more of the versatile tools in this powerful software.

No matter where you dip in you'll find great things to learn and explore at the turn of every page. You'll soon discover that making the most of your SMART Board is easier than you thought!

SECTION 3:
In the Driver's Seat—Build Pages from Scratch

Use a wider range of SMART Notebook tools and techniques.

Create new pages from scratch, following step-by-step video and written instructions.

Make the most dynamic, effective use of your SMART Board.

SECTION 4:
SMART Support for Your Journey

Reinforce your learning with a handy quick-reference guide to SMART Notebook tools and techniques.

Learn how to search for new ideas and activities on SMART Exchange and other websites.

You'll soon discover that making the most of your SMART Board is easier than you thought!

Section 1: Follow Along with Ready-to-Use Pages

Section 1 is all about getting your feet wet. In this section you'll find ready-to-use pages created with the SMART Notebook software that came with your board. Here, the goal is to focus on getting your SMART Board up and running throughout the day!

1 Activity Category: Scan quickly to find lessons for specific content areas: language arts, math, social studies, and science.

2 Check It Out!: Here's the website address for the online voice-over demonstration of how to use this activity page with your class. Type the address in the search bar of your Internet browser. (Take note! The addresses are case sensitive.) When the Web page for the voice-over demonstration opens, click on the Start triangle at the center of the screen. You may need to wait several seconds for the demonstration to begin.

3 Materials and Before You Begin: The activity pages I created for this book using SMART Notebook software are a fundamental part of the package. In fact, the first step in working with activities in Section 1 and Section 2 is to download the corresponding SMART Notebook file from the Internet. Each of these files is available through a unique website address listed here. Access the website as described above. When you click on the Start triangle, a dialog box will open, offering you the choice to save or open the file. Be sure *Save file* is selected, and click *OK*. The file will be saved to your Downloads folder.

Preparing and using the materials as described here will increase student interactivity.

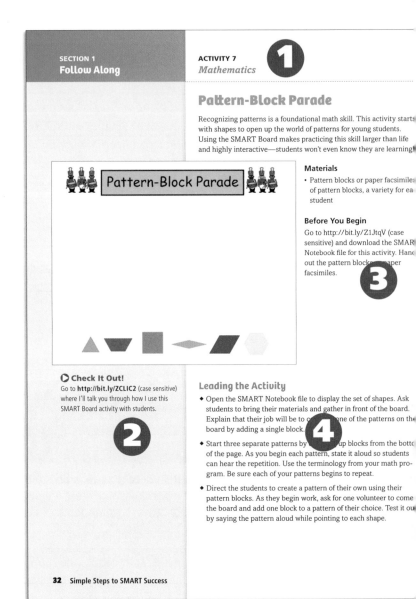

SECTION 1
Follow Along

ACTIVITY 7
Mathematics

1

Pattern-Block Parade

Recognizing patterns is a foundational math skill. This activity starts with shapes to open up the world of patterns for young students. Using the SMART Board makes practicing this skill larger than life and highly interactive—students won't even know they are learning!

Pattern-Block Parade

Materials
• Pattern blocks or paper facsimiles of pattern blocks, a variety for each student

Before You Begin
Go to http://bit.ly/Z1JtqV (case sensitive) and download the SMART Notebook file for this activity. Hand out the pattern blocks or paper facsimiles.

3

▶ **Check It Out!**
Go to **http://bit.ly/ZCLIC2** (case sensitive) where I'll talk you through how I use this SMART Board activity with students.

2

Leading the Activity
♦ Open the SMART Notebook file to display the set of shapes. Ask students to bring their materials and gather in front of the board. Explain that their job will be to continue one of the patterns on the board by adding a single block.

♦ Start three separate patterns by lining up blocks from the bottom of the page. As you begin each pattern, state it aloud so students can hear the repetition. Use the terminology from your math program. Be sure each of your patterns begins to repeat.

4

♦ Direct the students to create a pattern of their own using their pattern blocks. As they begin work, ask for one volunteer to come to the board and add one block to a pattern of their choice. Test it out by saying the pattern aloud while pointing to each shape.

32 Simple Steps to SMART Success

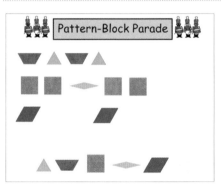

Pattern-Block Parade

» Occasionally, check in with individual students as they work; take time to discuss a pattern.

» Continue the activity until each child has had a chance to come to the board and add a block.

» When you're through, close the file by tapping on the x in the upper right corner of the screen. Tap on *No* in the pop-up window.

SMART Tip

As your students become more skilled at patterning, make the activity more complicated by changing the orientation of a block or making blocks touch each other along a common edge. To change the orientation of a block, tap it. Then tap the green button at the top of the frame around the shape and drag it clockwise or counterclockwise until it looks the way you want.

Behind the Curtain

I found the images for this activity by typing "pattern blocks" in the search box of the *Gallery* tab. Then I clicked on the *Pictures* bar. I dragged each image I wanted onto the page and resized it. Then I selected each image on the page and activated the *Infinite Cloner* option in that image's dropdown menu. This feature allows each block to be repeatedly reused during the activity. With the *Text* tool, I created a text box and typed the activity title in the box. I found the cute musician figures in the *Gallery* too, by searching the term "band."

④ **Leading the Activity:** Lead activities with greater ease by reviewing these instructions carefully from start to finish before you launch into an activity. Instructions include prompts for initiating conversation with your class to extend the learning.

⑤ **SMART Tip:** Look here for an extra tidbit, tip, or trick about using a SMART Board and SMART Notebook software.

⑥ **Behind the Curtain:** Here I explain which features of SMART Notebook software I used to build the page. These brief descriptions will help to familiarize you with SMART Notebook lingo. You'll notice right away that by using just one or two simple software tools, it's possible to create pages for highly engaging and fun activities. You'll be itching to start making SMART Board magic of your own!

Section 2: Get On Board with Interactive Templates

Section 2 provides your first glimpse into the wonderful interactive templates that already exist in the SMART Notebook software. Each activity in this part of the book is built upon a different template.

Pages in Section 2 are set up much the same as those in Section 1, but there are a few differences too.

1 Check It Out!: You'll find not one but *two* voice-over demonstrations for each Section 2 activity. One demonstration covers how to lead the activity; the second shows you how to add content to the interactive template to customize activities for your students. Follow the directions on page 8 to access these voice-over demonstrations. (Take note! The website addresses *are* case sensitive.)

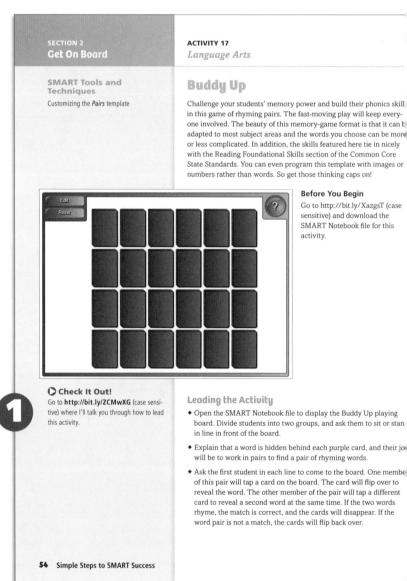

SMART Tools and Techniques

Customizing the *Pairs* template

Check It Out!
Go to **http://bit.ly/ZCMwXG** (case sensitive) where I'll talk you through how to lead this activity.

ACTIVITY 17
Language Arts

Buddy Up

Challenge your students' memory power and build their phonics skill in this game of rhyming pairs. The fast-moving play will keep everyone involved. The beauty of this memory-game format is that it can be adapted to most subject areas and the words you choose can be more or less complicated. In addition, the skills featured here tie in nicely with the Reading Foundational Skills section of the Common Core State Standards. You can even program this template with images or numbers rather than words. So get those thinking caps on!

Before You Begin
Go to http://bit.ly/XazgsT (case sensitive) and download the SMART Notebook file for this activity.

Leading the Activity

◆ Open the SMART Notebook file to display the Buddy Up playing board. Divide students into two groups, and ask them to sit or stand in line in front of the board.

◆ Explain that a word is hidden behind each purple card, and their job will be to work in pairs to find a pair of rhyming words.

◆ Ask the first student in each line to come to the board. One member of this pair will tap a card on the board. The card will flip over to reveal the word. The other member of the pair will tap a different card to reveal a second word at the same time. If the two words rhyme, the match is correct, and the cards will disappear. If the word pair is not a match, the cards will flip back over.

54 Simple Steps to SMART Success

Continue inviting pairs of students to the board in turn. As each correct pair is found, challenge your students to brainstorm other words that would rhyme with the pair or fit into its word family.

Play continues until time runs out or all cards have been matched.

When you're through, close the file by tapping on the x in the upper right corner of the screen. Tap on *No* in the pop-up window.

ow You're the Wizard

n the *Gallery* tab, click on *Lesson Activity Toolkit*. Click o̶ ̶ ̶ ̶e bar ̶tled *Interactive and Multimedia*. Scroll down to find one of the *Pairs* ̶mplates. Double-click or drag and drop the template onto your ̶MART Notebook page. Click on the *Edit* button. Now you can decide ̶ow many pairs you want to include and add content to each card.

̶lick on the card you want to start with and type a word or drag and ̶op an image. Continue with the other cards. Whatever you type or ̶ace on card number 1, be sure to type or place the matching content ̶n the other card numbered 1. To edit any text, click and highlight ̶ then edit as you would if you were word processing. Once you've ̶nished, click the *Ok* button. Name and save the file.

Think of the Possibilities

A memory-game format can be adapted to practice almost any skill with any age group. Traditional matches can consist of identical images, letters, words, or numbers.

Nontraditional matches might consist of a number and a mathematical expression that equals that number, a word and its part of speech or definition, two homonyms, two synonyms, two antonyms, a story element and a text detail from the story, or even two objects that belong to the same category. Be creative!

SMART Tip

In this template, you have the option of numbering the tiles. When you are using many pairs, numbered tiles may help students keep track of the location of certain words more readily. If students are a little more advanced in skill, they might like the challenge of unnumbered tiles. You can change this at any time by tapping the *Edit* button and checking or unchecking *Show tile numbers*.

▶ **Check It Out!**
Go to **http://bit.ly/YtDfTY** (case sensitive) where I'll explain how to work with the *Pairs* template.

②Think of the Possibilities:
To help stimulate your creative thinking, check out these ideas on how to adapt the template and the activity to add challenge or delve into other content areas. Once you understand how a template works, get your brain juicing about how to use it throughout your school day. SMART Notebook templates are incredibly versatile!

③Now You're the Wizard:
Start exercising your power by following these instructions for customizing a template. You'll be surprised and delighted as you discover how quickly and easily you can create dynamic and varied class activities simply by typing text or adding objects to a template. As I said earlier, *you* are the source of the magic in your classroom.

Section 3: In the Driver's Seat— Build Pages from Scratch

Here's where you'll really dive in, creating your own SMART Board pages and activities using a combination of SMART Notebook tools and techniques plus the incredible wealth of images and other goodies in the SMART Notebook *Gallery*. Of course, I still provide instructions for leading the activity, but look what else you'll find:

❶ SMART Tools and Techniques: Look here to see which tools and techniques you'll learn as you build the page for this activity. Early on, the activities primarily use the most basic tools. As you progress, you'll master additional skills and techniques to expand your bag of SMART magic tricks.

❷ Check It Out!: Follow along with one voice-over demonstration on leading the activity and another that shows you exactly how I created each SMART Notebook page, step by step. Follow the directions on page 8 to access these voice-over demonstrations. Remember that the website addresses *are* case sensitive.

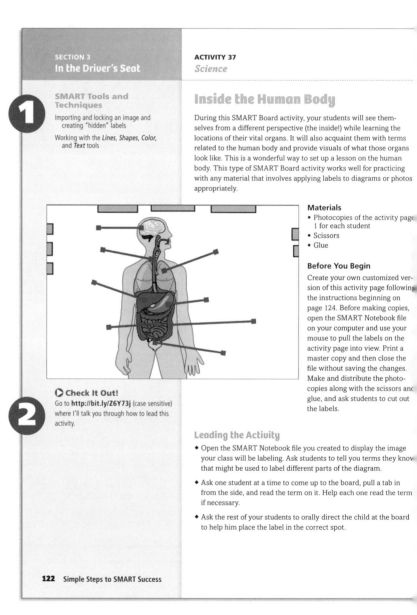

SECTION 3
In the Driver's Seat

❶

SMART Tools and Techniques

Importing and locking an image and creating "hidden" labels

Working with the *Lines, Shapes, Color,* and *Text* tools

▶ Check It Out!
Go to **http://bit.ly/Z6Y73j** (case sensitive) where I'll talk you through how to lead this activity.

❷

ACTIVITY 37
Science

Inside the Human Body

During this SMART Board activity, your students will see themselves from a different perspective (the inside!) while learning the locations of their vital organs. It will also acquaint them with terms related to the human body and provide visuals of what those organs look like. This is a wonderful way to set up a lesson on the human body. This type of SMART Board activity works well for practicing with any material that involves applying labels to diagrams or photos appropriately.

Materials
• Photocopies of the activity page 1 for each student
• Scissors
• Glue

Before You Begin

Create your own customized version of this activity page following the instructions beginning on page 124. Before making copies, open the SMART Notebook file on your computer and use your mouse to pull the labels on the activity page into view. Print a master copy and then close the file without saving the changes. Make and distribute the photocopies along with the scissors and glue, and ask students to cut out the labels.

Leading the Activity

◆ Open the SMART Notebook file you created to display the image your class will be labeling. Ask students to tell you terms they know that might be used to label different parts of the diagram.

◆ Ask one student at a time to come up to the board, pull a tab in from the side, and read the term on it. Help each one read the term if necessary.

◆ Ask the rest of your students to orally direct the child at the board to help him place the label in the correct spot.

122 Simple Steps to SMART Success

Building the *Inside the Human Body* Page

⊙ **Check It Out!**
Go to **http://bit.ly/YdNedJ** (case sensitive) where I'll talk you
through how to build this SMART Notebook page step by step.

1. Open a new SMART Notebook file by double-
   clicking on the SMART Notebook icon on your
   desktop.

2. Click on the *Gallery* tab. In the search box, type
   a phrase related to whatever content you plan to
   study. If you want to create a page like my example, type "inside the body." Click on the magnifying
   glass that is just to the right of the search box. The
   results of your search will appear near the middle
   of the tab in the form of blue bars. Click on the blue
   bar that says *Pictures*. For this example, choose the
   Inside the body image.

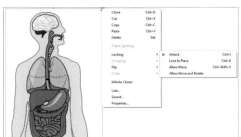

3. Double-click on the image or
   drag and drop it onto the page.
   Click, drag, and drop it into
   position. If needed, click on
   the image again so that a blue
   frame appears around it. Then
   click on the gray menu arrow
   in the upper right corner and
   choose *Locking* and then *Lock
   In Place*. This will prevent the
   body image from being accidentally moved out of position
   when students are moving the
   labels. We certainly don't want
   the intestines to end up where
   the brain should be!

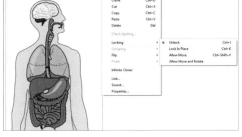

Simple Steps to SMART Success

---

❸ **Building the Page:** Build your software knowledge and skills with these
in-depth tutorial guides to using SMART
Notebook. Starting from the very beginning—opening a new file in the software—
these instructions walk you through every
detail of creating a SMART Notebook
activity page. Along the way, I point out
the specific icons for the tools used and the
options to select from drop-down menus.
Remember that you can follow along with
the voice-over demonstrations too, which
show you precisely what you'll be seeing
on your computer screen as you work.

Section 4: SMART Support for Your Journey

Learning about and using new computer software can leave you feeling a little overwhelmed and isolated. In this section of the book, I supply an illustrated glossary where you can find fast answers to questions about using SMART Notebook software. Plus, I pave the road for you to the friendly, knowledge-able, and lively online community of SMART Board users. Turn here to find:

◆ A quick-reference Wizard's Guide to all of the individual SMART Notebook tools and techniques mentioned in this book

◆ A list of my favorite lessons from SMART Exchange™

◆ Some sites to check out for more SMART Board lessons and ideas

◆ Navigation tips for each site

I know you will find that each section of this book will bring your SMART Board skills to life and increase your students' excitement about learning. I wish you many happy adventures as you continue to explore the world of SMART con-nections while introducing this exciting technology to your classroom.

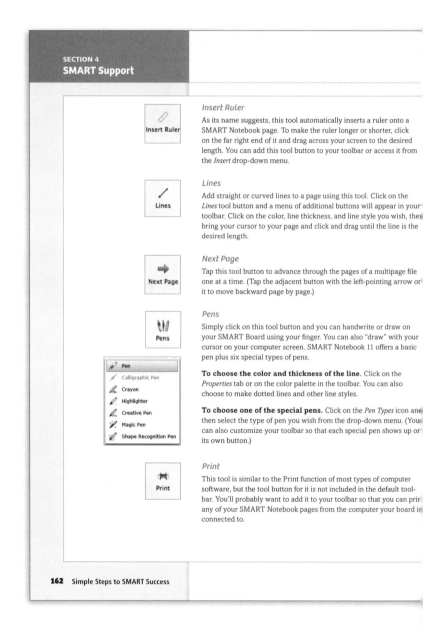

Working with the SMART Board and SMART Notebook Software

You and your SMART Board are going to be great friends—I just know it! However, it will take some planning and trial and error to figure out how to make a SMART Board a natural part of your teaching. To help you develop a good working relationship with your SMART Board, I've compiled my best advice, tips, and tricks to save you time and energy in areas such as managing your classroom during SMART Board activities; saving, locating, and opening SMART Notebook files; importing images into SMART Notebook files; updating your software (it's free!); and customizing the SMART Notebook toolbar so that all of your favorite software tools will be right at your fingertips. You'll also see how easily your SMART Board can help you tackle some of the Common Core State Standards and National Educational Technology Standards.

Classroom Management During SMART Board Activities

In my instructions for leading activities, I've kept the focus on the task your students will be performing, the rules of play for team games, and methods of keeping activities interactive. But whenever you introduce a SMART Board activity, keep in mind these general management and instructional tidbits that might help you along the way:

◆ Each time you invite your students to come to the board as a group, remind them to find a spot where they have a clear view of the board. And if they'll be writing or using manipulatives, they'll need to allow some floor space for that too, and they may want to bring along a notebook or some other hard surface to write on.

◆ When activities call for dividing students into teams, I simply designated them Team One and Team Two, but I know you'll be more creative than that! Your students will love coming up with names for their teams— names related to seasonal events are always popular. Who wouldn't want to be on the Base-Ten Bats team or a member of the Wily Word Wizards?

◆ Having students work in pairs is a powerful educational technique, especially during math activities. It gives students a chance to share problem-solving approaches and ideas and communicate using subject-specific terms. Some activities in this book are designed specifically as partner activities, but many others could be adapted for partner interaction too. Get your "grouping cap" on! If you think an activity can work as a partner activity, go for it!

You and your SMART Board are going to be great friends—I just know it!

◆ Some activities call for students to manipulate paper versions of the objects on the screen. When that's the case, you'll need to print a master copy of the activity page and make photocopies ahead of time, and black-and-white photocopies are sufficient for the most part. If individual objects (such as the weather symbols in What's the Weather? on page 80) need to be cut apart, organize your students to do this during the activity itself or as a separate step before the activity begins. It helps develop their fine-motor skills, and it will save you time.

◆ When possible, in some way, shape, or form, whatever is happening at the board should also be happening out in your "audience," so to speak. For example, when one of your students is manipulating fraction pieces on the SMART Board, I hope you'll prompt the rest of your class to do the same using paper pieces. I've included this interactive step in the directions for leading many of the activities in the book, and I encourage you to look for interactive potential in every activity you create yourself using the SMART Notebook software.

Managing SMART Files with Ease

Two of the most common questions I field from classroom teachers are: How do I open a new SMART Notebook file? Where in the world do my SMART Notebook files go when I save them?

Here are the answers to these questions, along with a few other tips for efficient file management. Don't worry—soon you will be opening, saving, and retrieving SMART Notebook files with ease.

Opening a New SMART Notebook File

This one is a piece of cake! When SMART Notebook software was installed on your computer, a blue-and-white SMART Notebook icon should have appeared on your desktop. Do you see it? To open a new file, all you have to do is double-click that icon. It's just like double-clicking on the Microsoft Word icon on your desktop when you want to type a letter or other document.

Saving and Locating SMART Notebook Files

Once you've created a page using the SMART Notebook software, you'll need to save it. Saving one of these files is just like saving any other file you've ever created. When you are ready to close the file, you will click the x in the upper right corner of your screen. A pop-up window will appear, asking whether you want to save the changes you made. If you're closing a brand-new SMART Notebook file, first click *Yes* or *Save*. At this point, a dialog box should appear and you get to tell your computer where to save the file.

Now, where you choose to save this file and what you choose to call it are up to you, but don't get too clever here or you might outsmart yourself! I mean, have you ever saved something and then not been able to find it later? I have. If you've created a complex activity page, you'll have invested some serious time doing so, and you'll certainly want to be able to find the page again later on! So, when that dialog box appears, don't just hit *Save*. Look at the top of that box. It tells you which directory the file will be saved in. If you don't like what's listed there, change it before you hit *Save*.

The dialog box will display all of the choices for places to save your work: documents, pictures, videos, desktop, and so on. Click on the one that corresponds to where you want to save the file, name the file something reasonable and easy to remember (here's where the outsmarting yourself can happen), and then click *Save* at the bottom of the box. I usually recommend saving to your Documents folder. I strongly recommend NOT saving each individual file to your desktop. In my work coaching teachers, I have seen computer desktop displays that were pretty scary! Although it seems as though the desktop is the easiest place to find something, I encourage you to break the habit. It will come back to haunt you later when you can't find anything in the icon jungle on your desktop. You might, however, decide to create a folder especially for all of your SMART Notebook activity pages and lessons and create one desktop shortcut for that folder. Every time you save a file, make sure you save it to that particular folder. It will be easy to find whenever you need it!

Reopening a Saved File

Opening a SMART Notebook file is just like opening any type of file. First click on the desktop shortcut to the folder where you keep your SMART Notebook files. Double-click on the name of the file you want to open. It might take a few moments to open, depending on how large the file is. Pages created in SMART Notebook are generally bigger pieces of information for your computer to read than a regular Word document, so give it time. Clicking again and again will actually make it go slower, so avoid the urge—leave the room if you need to!

Now that you have created, named, saved, and reopened a file, there's just one more thing to know. When you open a file on the SMART Board and lead an activity with your students, it may be best *not* to save changes when you're done. If your students were dragging, dropping, writing, rotating, matching . . . or doing anything else that changed the original layout of the page, don't save the changes. That way, when you open up the file for use in the future, it will be unchanged and ready for immediate use. Choose to save only if you want the changes made on that page to become part of the permanent layout.

SMART Tip

Downloading the SMART Notebook files for the activities in the book is easy to do. Simply open your Web browser and type in the appropriate website name exactly as it appears in the Before You Begin section of the activity. (Note that this is case sensitive.) Hit enter. When you get to the Web page, just follow the instructions on page 8 for downloading the file.

Customizing Your Toolbar

Another common question I field in my work as a consultant is, Why do I need to customize my toolbar? Ease of use or efficiency is the primary reason to add or delete tools from your toolbar. As you learn more about the tools and what they do, some will really tickle your interest. You'll want the tools that you use most often to be available at your fingertips (literally). Those are tools you'll want to add to your default toolbar (the one that shows as soon as you open SMART Notebook). Other tools will leave you thinking, When would I ever use that? It's best just to remove those from your toolbar. They're taking up valuable dashboard space. Get rid of them. You can always bring them back on board later if you wish.

If you are working in SMART Notebook Version 11, look at the upper right corner of your toolbar on any SMART page, and you should see a small cog or gear. Clicking on that icon will give you access to the entire SMART Notebook toolbox.

If you're not working in SMART Notebook 11 (or even if you are), there's another way to gain access to the big toolbox. Simply click on the *View* menu in the upper left corner of the page. Select *Customize Toolbar*, which is just past halfway down in the drop-down menu. A pop-up window with the entire toolbox in it will appear.

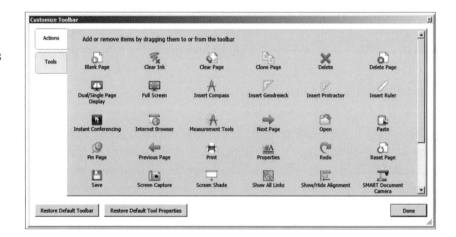

SMART Tip

Some of the buttons on your toolbar display a small black upside-down triangle either before or after you click on them. This is a universal symbol in the software that means "there's more." So, if you see that little triangle, click on it. It will likely give you more options (such as more shapes or colors) for the tool you are currently working with.

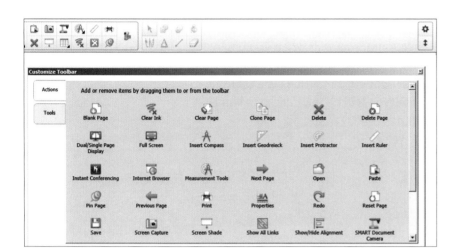

To add a tool: Click and drag the tool(s) you want directly into your toolbar at the top of your SMART page—you can drop a tool in any part of the toolbar that does not appear washed out.

Once you're done, click the *Done* button in the bottom right corner of the toolbox.

To delete a tool: Click and drag the tool you do not want out of the toolbar at the top of your SMART page and drop it anywhere in the big toolbox. Repeat for any other tools you do not want. Click the *Done* button in the bottom right corner of the toolbox when you're finished.

Another new feature of Version 11 is that some of the tools have been compacted or combined. For example, the *Pens* tool has lots of other pens "inside" it (click on the *Pens* tool icon to reveal these). Some folks like this compact design, but if you don't, there's an easy fix. Each of the writing tools inside the *Pens* tool also has a separate button in the big toolbox. While customizing your toolbar, you can drag any or all of these specific pens, such as the *Highlighter Pen*, up to your toolbar. The same is true with most of the options inside the *View Screens* tool.

Importing Images

Even though the SMART Notebook software has over 5,000 images in its *Gallery*, you will likely want to look for other sources as well when you begin to create your own pages, games, and lessons. The Internet is full of images that can be located using a search engine like Google. Please be sure that the images you use are copyright free; otherwise, you will be infringing on someone else's property and actually violating the copyright law. You can find copyright-free images online by including the words "copyright-free images" along with your search term. Try this, and you'll find links to many sites that offer such photos for use by the public. For example, the website Pics4Learning (www.pics4learning.com) offers what are called copyright-friendly images, which are made available specifically for student and teacher use in print, video, or other multimedia creations. You can also import images from clip art programs you may have purchased for other purposes. Both are easy to do and will open up the possibilities for your board even more!

Once you've imported an image from the Internet or a clip art file, it should appear on your SMART Notebook page with a blue frame around it. You can make it bigger or smaller by using the resize button in the lower right corner of the frame. To move the image around on the page, click on it and drag and drop it.

Importing images from the Internet:

1. Go to a search engine like Google or Yahoo.
2. Click on the word *Images* near the top of the page.
3. Type your search term in the search box and hit *Enter*.
4. Scroll down until you find an image you like.
5. Right-click on the image (Mac users, *Ctrl* and click).
6. Select *Copy Image* from the drop-down menu.
7. Go back to your SMART Notebook page in progress.
8. Right-click on the page.
9. Select *Paste* from the drop-down menu.

Importing images from a clip art program:

1. Open the clip art program.
2. Find the image you want to use.
3. Right-click on that image.
4. Select *Copy*.
5. Return to your SMART Notebook page in progress.
6. Right-click on the page.
7. Select *Paste*.

Keeping Yourself Up to Date

Occasionally, SMART Technologies updates the SMART Notebook software. In any update, features are usually added, but sometimes features are also changed or taken away. The good news is that when SMART Technologies updates the software, you receive that update for free, and the update includes a tutorial that takes you through what's new or different. Both of these options are available to you at any time.

If you are working on a school-owned computer, you may need to check with someone about updating because a password might be involved.

If you've recently updated and want to review the tutorial for that version, click on *Help* at the top of any SMART Notebook page. Select *Tutorial* from the drop-down menu. It's definitely worth the 30 minutes or so it takes to watch the tutorial, and you can revisit it at any time.

Updating SMART Notebook Software on Your Computer

1. Open a new SMART Notebook file.

2. Click on the *Help* menu at the top (left) of the page.

3. Select *Check for Updates and Activation*.

4. A pop-up window will appear that says *Smart Product Update* with a blue bar at the bottom. This means it's checking your current software. (Note: You'll need to be connected to the Internet for this to work.)

5. If part of your software needs to be updated, a new dialog box will appear with active *Update* buttons next to the items that are in need of update.

6. Click on the items you wish to update—most likely *Notebook, Gallery Essentials*, and/or *Lesson Activity Toolkit*.

7. Ask someone at your organization before updating other items, such as *Product Drivers* or *Common Files*.

SMART and the Standards

The Common Core State Standards are on everyone's mind these days. The good news here is that many of the activities that you'll use and make under the guidance of this book address Common Core expectations. Here are just a few examples:

ACTIVITY TITLE	COMMON CORE STATE STANDARD ADDRESSED
Adjective Arranger *page 27*	1.SL.4, 1.L.5, 2.L.6, 3.RL.4, 3.L.4, 3.L.6
How Many Sounds? *page 28*	1.RFS.3, 2.RFS.3, 3.RFS.3
Place-Value Diamonds *page 40*	1.NBT.1, 1.NBT.5, 2.NBT.1, 2.NBT.4
How's Your Memory? *page 42*	1.RFS.4, 1.L.2, 2.RFS.3, 2.RFS.4, 3.RFS.4
Match My Expression *page 64*	1.OA.2, 1.OA.7, 2.OA.1, 2.OA.2
Roll and Write *page 68*	2.NBT.3, 3.OA.1, 3.NBT.1
Complex Shape Sort *page 92*	1.G.1, 2.G.1, 3.G.1
Word-Choice Wonders *page 112*	1.RL.7, 1.L.6, 2.RL.7, 2.L.4, 3.RL.7, 3.L.6

The activities in this book also address a set of standards you might not even know about—the National Educational Technology Standards (NETS) put forth by the International Society for Technology in Education (ISTE). There's a set for students and a set for teachers. They can be found at www.iste.org/standards if you want to take a peek. As the creator of pages for your SMART Board, you'll be addressing NETS standards such as Design and Develop Digital Age Learning Experiences and Modeling Digital Age Work and Learning. As your students become greater consumers of and producers on the SMART Board, you'll be helping them reach the Communication and Collaboration and Research and Information Fluency standards, to name just a few.

Follow Along with Ready-to-Use Pages

Welcome! I designed this section of the book with ready-to-use SMART Notebook pages especially for the Nervous Novice. (Don't worry, though. Even an advanced SMART Board user will find activities here that her students will enjoy.) Each activity is based on a SMART page I created using SMART Notebook software.

To use any of these activities in your classroom, all you have to do is download and open the corresponding SMART Notebook file—the Web address where you can access the appropriate file is given under the Before You Begin heading of each activity. Leading the Activity provides all the instructions for engaging your students in the activity. And for those who prefer to learn by observing, I've created voice-over demonstrations—including special bonus ideas for extending each lesson—that you can access online. (Check It Out! provides the Web address for each demonstration.)

Behind the Curtain is a description of the SMART Notebook tools and techniques I used to build the page. Some pages were a snap to create, and you'll find those right at the start of this section of the book. As you progress through Section 1, you'll find SMART pages that were built with a wider range of the software's tools and techniques. You'll be delighted to see how easy it is to use the software to create great lessons that emphasize a diverse array of skills, from reading maps and understanding place value to choosing adjectives and using money. (If you're new to SMART Notebook software and are curious about some of the tools and techniques I mention, take a look at the Wizard's Guide on page 160. It's a convenient and quick tutorial for newbies.) SMART Tips are simple tricks for using your SMART Board while leading the activity, or a variation on the basic lesson format. So go ahead, dig in, enjoy, and start realizing the power of your SMART Notebook software!

Nervous Novices start here to learn the basics of working with a SMART Board and the software.

Number Sense-ation

Good number sense includes a solid grasp of number patterns and relationships. Frequent practice with numbers in a visual format like a chart will help students actually *see* the math you are talking about. This activity ties nicely into the Operations and Algebraic Thinking expectations for kindergarten and first grade found in the Common Core State Standards. The interactive format makes this a great match for your active learners too!

1	2	3	4	5	6	7	8	9	10
11	12	13	14	15	16	17	18	19	20
21	22	23	24	25	26	27	28	29	30
31	32	33	34	35	36	37	38	39	40
41	42	43	44	45	46	47	48	49	50
51	52	53	54	55	56	57	58	59	60
61	62	63	64	65	66	67	68	69	70
71	72	73	74	75	76	77	78	79	80
81	82	83	84	85	86	87	88	89	90
91	92	93	94	95	96	97	98	99	100

Display multiples of [ ] ☐ Zero-based **RESET**

Materials
- Photocopies of the activity page, 1 for each student
- Transparent plastic bingo chips or highlighting tape

Before You Begin
Go to http://bit.ly/YbxD1p (case sensitive) and download the SMART Notebook file for this activity. Distribute the photocopies and bingo chips or highlighting tape.

▶ **Check It Out!**
Go to **http://bit.ly/151UAnR** (case sensitive) where I'll talk you through how I use this SMART Board activity with students.

Leading the Activity

◆ Open the SMART Notebook file to display the hundred square. Ask students to bring their materials and gather in front of the board. Demonstrate how the hundred square works: Tap a number, and the tile flips over and turns red. Tap it again, and it flips back and turns gray. Tap several squares, and show that you can turn the entire hundred square back to gray by pressing the *Reset* button in the lower right corner.

◆ Explain that you will pose a problem, and they will solve it using the hundred square. Work through an example or two first, such as

"I am on the number 38." (Tap the 38 tile.) "I decrease by 6. Where am I now?" Here's a second example: "I start on the number 46." (Tap the 46 tile.) "If I increase by 3 spaces, would I land on an odd number or an even number?"

- Pose a problem and ask a student to come to the board to figure out the answer. Ask the rest of the class to figure it out on their own using their papers and chips and to signal you when they have a response. If you wish, students can work in pairs to figure out the responses. (Each pair will need one small dry-erase board and a dry-erase marker.) They can discuss and solve the problem together, then display their answer on the dry-erase board.

- Ask the student at the board to demonstrate and explain how he arrived at his answer.

- Repeat with other problems that are appropriate for your students.

- When you're through, close the file by tapping on the x in the upper right corner of the screen. Tap on *No* in the pop-up window.

The *Gallery* tab of SMART Notebook software is a gold mine of resources. To find the number grid I used for this activity, I typed "hundred square" in the search box of the *Gallery* tab and then selected this one from the *Interactive and Multimedia* category. I double-clicked on the thumbnail in the *Gallery* tab, and voilà, it was instantly copied onto the blank page I'd opened up. Then all I had to do was name and save the file.

SMART Tip

Be sure to use a variety of mathematical vocabulary. Besides using the terms *forward* and *backward*, use *added* and *subtracted*, and words or phrases from word problems, such as *sum, product,* and *difference.* Ask students to show traditional or complex skip counting/multiplication patterns or to start at a particular number and tell you what the next number would be if you were counting by 5s, for example. You can also pose mixed-operation problems.

1	2	3	4	5	6	7	8	9	10
11	12	13	14	15	16	17	18	19	20
21	22	23	24	25	26	27	28	29	30
31	32	33	34	35	36	37	38	39	40
41	42	43	44	45	46	47	48	49	50
51	52	53	54	55	56	57	58	59	60
61	62	63	64	65	66	67	68	69	70
71	72	73	74	75	76	77	78	79	80
81	82	83	84	85	86	87	88	89	90
91	92	93	94	95	96	97	98	99	100

Display multiples of ___ ☐ Zero-based RESET

At the Fair

You and your students will be craving cotton candy when you're done with this activity, which focuses on the fairgrounds and directional language: words such as *between*, *farthest*, and *above*. Everyone's involved and there's plenty to do, so grab your tickets!

Materials

- Photocopies of the activity page, 1 for each student
- Multicolored crayons or markers

Before You Begin

Go to http://bit.ly/WJNOF1 (case sensitive) and download the SMART Notebook file for this activity. Distribute the photocopies and crayons or markers.

▶ Check It Out!

Go to **http://bit.ly/ZqVUiz** (case sensitive) where I'll talk you through how I use this SMART Board activity with students.

SMART Tip

Try this activity with the image of your choice. In the *Gallery*, do searches using terms such as "pancake breakfast," "playground," and "living room," and then click on *Notebook Files and Pages* to see what SMART Notebook has to offer.

Behind the Curtain

Are you wondering how I drew this beautiful page? Gotcha! SMART Notebook drew it for me. All I did was type "fair" in the search box of *Gallery Essentials* and then select *Notebook Files and Pages*. This image is called *Fair*. I double-clicked on the *Fair* thumbnail, and I was ready to go.

Leading the Activity

◆ Open the SMART Notebook file to show the fair scene. Ask students to bring their materials and gather in front of the board. Explain that their job is to listen to and follow your directions about adding specific items to the picture.

◆ Ask for a volunteer to come to the board. Give the first direction, such as "Add a yellow flag to the top of the carousel." Tell the student at the board to use the *Pen* tool and assist him if necessary in changing the ink color to yellow. Allow all students time to draw; check in with them as they work. Check with the student at the board as well. If there is any confusion, model the action at the board.

◆ Repeat with other volunteers and other directions, such as "Put a blue x on the tent that is farthest away. Draw a person on the third carousel horse. Draw a green trash can next to the biggest tent. Add an orange bird above the smallest tent. Draw a purple square around the center of the Ferris wheel. Add a ticket booth between the big tent and the carousel. Make a red line to the left of the Ferris wheel."

◆ When you're through, close the file by tapping on the x in the upper right corner of the screen. Tap on *No* in the pop-up window.

Adjective Arranger

Mastering a broad vocabulary will improve your students' skills in writing and reading comprehension, so anytime you can use sophisticated words with your students, you should! This engaging activity combines a bit of critical thinking and Common Core Language expectations with interesting images and words. The conversations can be just as interactive as the work on the board, so don't skimp on them. Your students will love it!

Before You Begin

Go to http://bit.ly/YsUchl (case sensitive) and download the SMART Notebook file for this activity.

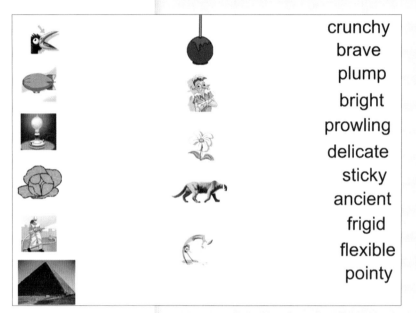

crunchy
brave
plump
bright
prowling
delicate
sticky
ancient
frigid
flexible
pointy

Leading the Activity

◆ Open the SMART Notebook file to display the images and adjectives. Ask students to join you in front of the board. Tell them that their job is to match each adjective with the image it best describes. Point out that some of the adjectives could be matched with more than one image. Read aloud each word, and name each image.

◆ Call your students' attention to the first picture and ask them to help you decide which word best matches it. Drag that adjective over and drop it next to the image.

◆ Tell your students that their next job will be to find something else in the room that can be described using the same adjective, or to brainstorm with you about other objects that could be described that way. (The action part will depend on the adjective. You likely have pointy things in your classroom but not something ancient— unless your students consider you to be so!)

◆ If you plan to send your students off to explore the room, first demonstrate a signal you'll use when you want students to stop and pay attention. Let them start exploring. Allow them time to find an object and then give your signal. As a group, discuss some of their choices.

◆ Repeat the process until each image has been assigned an adjective.

◆ When you're through, close the file by tapping on the x in the upper right corner of the screen. Tap on *No* in the pop-up window.

▶ **Check It Out!**

Go to **http://bit.ly/XaB5Gm** (case sensitive) where I'll talk you through how I use this SMART Board activity with students.

SMART Tip

Because the goal of this activity is to expand vocabulary, it's okay (even better, actually!) if your students are not familiar with or cannot read the adjectives I've chosen.

Behind the Curtain

Here's another page made using the *Text* tool and *Gallery* images. I first found all the images in the *Gallery Essentials* section and put them on the page, figured out a set of adjectives that would match up, and typed them in random order on the page.

How Many Sounds?

Phonics and phonemic awareness are the foundation of all reading and writing, but practicing those skills can be kind of . . . boring. Using your SMART Board and asking students to step into the role of judges for this activity will make a big difference in student investment. This activity includes both pictures and words, so it works well for students of all abilities. Plus, it will help your students meet some of the Reading Foundational Skills set out in the Common Core State Standards.

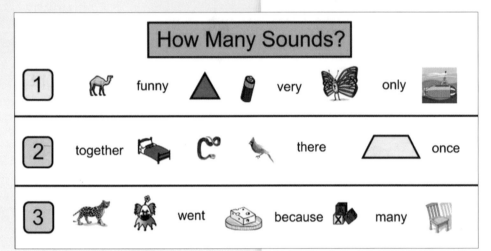

Materials
• Index cards, 1 for each student
• Colored pens or crayons

Before You Begin

Go to http://bit.ly/WpR2ev (case sensitive) and download the SMART Notebook file for this activity. Hand out the index cards, and ask your students to draw a smiley face on one side of the card and a sad face on the other.

▶ Check It Out!
Go to **http://bit.ly/WK6K6E** (case sensitive) where I'll talk you through how I use this SMART Board activity with students.

SMART Tip

While this activity uses a combination of both pictures and words, remember that you always have the option of creating a page using images only, or text only, depending on what's appropriate for the age and ability of your students.

Leading the Activity

◆ Open the SMART Notebook file to display the rows of objects and words. Ask students to bring their cards and gather in front of the board. Explain that they will be listening for the number of chunks, or syllables, in each word or picture. The number of syllables should match the number at the left-hand end of the row. Their job will be to choose a picture or word that is in the wrong row and drag it to the correct row.

◆ Name each image and read each word.

◆ Ask for a volunteer to come to the board and make the first change. Once she has moved an image or word, ask your students to vote using their index cards. If they agree with the item moved, they should show the smiley-face side of the card. If they disagree, they should show the sad face.

- After your students vote, confirm whether the move is correct. If it isn't, ask your students for advice on how to fix it.

- Repeat the process, inviting a different student to the board each time, until all items are in the correct row.

- When you're through, close the file by tapping on the x in the upper right corner of the screen. Tap on *No* in the pop-up window.

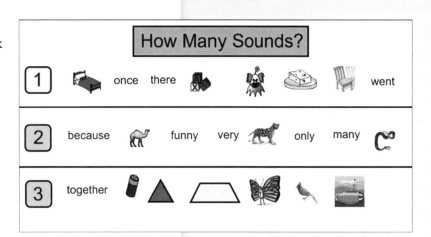

Behind the Curtain

To make the three-row format for this page, I used the *Lines* tool in the toolbar. All of the images on this page come straight from the *Gallery Essentials* section of the *Gallery* tab. I just browsed to find images that were age-appropriate. I dragged and dropped them on the page, then used the *Text* tool to create the title and add the words between the images.

ACTIVITY 5
Science

Habitat Homes

Learning about animal habitats is extra fun when your SMART Board is part of the action. This page works well for a whole-group activity or for centers.

Materials
- Photocopies of the activity page, 1 for each student
- Scissors
- Glue

Before You Begin

Go to http://bit.ly/16uFWJd (case sensitive) and download the SMART Notebook file for this activity. Distribute the photocopies along with the scissors and glue.

▶ Check It Out!

Go to **http://bit.ly/ZQjp6A** (case sensitive) where I'll talk you through how I use this SMART Board activity with students.

Behind the Curtain

My first step in making this page was to type "lake" in the search box of the *Gallery*. I dragged and dropped the thumbnail of the pond onto the blank page and resized it. Then I searched for the various animals and added them in the same way. I used the *Text* tool to add the labels, and I used the *Grouping* technique to "glue" the images and labels together. To make the activity self-checking, I applied the *Lock In Place* option in the drop-down menus of the images of animals that do not live in a pond.

Leading the Activity

◆ Open the SMART Notebook file to display the pond and animals. Ask students to bring their materials and gather in front of the board. Explain that their job is to decide which animals live in the pond and which do not. Read aloud the name of each animal.

◆ Ask for a volunteer to come to the board and drag an image of an animal to the pond. If the animal chosen is a pond dweller, the image will move easily. If the animal is not a pond dweller, the image will not move. Invite the rest of the class to cut out the picture of the pond-dwelling animal and paste it onto the pond on their papers.

◆ Try enlarging an image of an animal to point out features that make it well adapted to pond life. Simply tap the image and then touch and drag the resize button that appears in the lower right corner. (P.S. The software won't let you resize the "locked" images.)

◆ Repeat until all the pond dwellers have been moved to the pond. (There should be 10 animals in the pond.)

◆ When you're through, close the file by tapping on the x in the upper right corner of the screen. Tap on *No* in the pop-up window.

Land (and Water) Ho!

Play a guessing game that gives your students an opportunity to enhance their geography, collaboration, and teamwork skills all at once! This activity works nicely as a review or as an informal pre-assessment before a unit on map skills.

Materials
- Set of 13 index cards, 6 labeled "land" and 7 labeled "water"
- Opaque bag

Before You Begin

Go to http://bit.ly/WpRk5e (case sensitive) and download the SMART Notebook file for this activity. Place the set of index cards in the opaque bag.

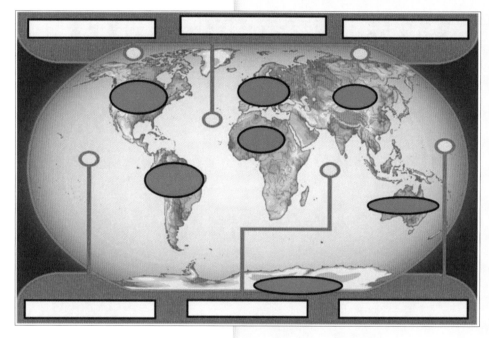

Leading the Activity

- Open the file to display the world map. Ask students to join you in front of the board. Explain that their job will be to work in pairs to identify a land or water feature on the map. Point out the orange ovals and yellow rectangles, and explain that they are covering up the names of continents and bodies of water.

- Divide your students into two teams. Arrange teams in two single-file lines facing the board. Explain that two players from each team will collaborate during their turn.

- To start play, ask the first player from Team One to pick a card. Invite that player and the second student in line to discuss and correctly identify a land or water feature (according to which type of card was picked) and then drag away the oval or rectangle to check whether their guess is correct. If it is, their team gets a point. If it isn't correct, the other team gets a point.

- Play continues, with teams alternating turns. When all of the features have been identified, the team with the most points wins the game.

- When you're through, close the file by tapping on the x in the upper right corner of the screen. Tap on *No* in the pop-up window.

▶ Check It Out!

Go to **http://bit.ly/YtrWez** (case sensitive) where I'll talk you through how I use this SMART Board activity with students.

SMART Tip

It's so easy to insert any image or template you find in the *Gallery* onto a SMART Notebook page. Just drag and drop it or double-click it!

Behind the Curtain

I created this graphic using a pre-labeled map I found in the *Geography* section of the *Gallery* tab. All I had to do was use the *Shapes* tool to create the ovals and rectangles. Then I worked with the *Color* tool to fill the shapes with opaque colors and thus hide the labels from view.

Pattern-Block Parade

Recognizing patterns is a foundational math skill. This activity starts with shapes to open up the world of patterns for young students. Using the SMART Board makes practicing this skill larger than life and highly interactive—students won't even know they are learning!

 Pattern-Block Parade

Materials

- Pattern blocks or paper facsimiles of pattern blocks, a variety for each student

Before You Begin

Go to http://bit.ly/Z1JtqV (case sensitive) and download the SMART Notebook file for this activity. Hand out the pattern blocks or paper facsimiles.

▶ **Check It Out!**

Go to **http://bit.ly/ZCLIC2** (case sensitive) where I'll talk you through how I use this SMART Board activity with students.

Leading the Activity

◆ Open the SMART Notebook file to display the set of shapes. Ask students to bring their materials and gather in front of the board. Explain that their job will be to continue one of the patterns on the board by adding a single block.

◆ Start three separate patterns by dragging up blocks from the bottom of the page. As you begin each pattern, state it aloud so students can hear the repetition. Use the terminology from your math program. Be sure each of your patterns begins to repeat.

◆ Direct the students to create a pattern of their own using their pattern blocks. As they begin work, ask for one volunteer to come to the board and add one block to a pattern of their choice. Test it out by saying the pattern aloud while pointing to each shape.

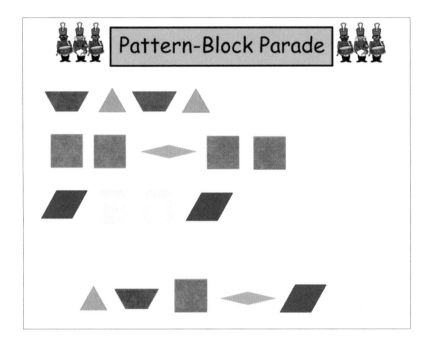

- Occasionally, check in with individual students as they work; take time to discuss a pattern.

- Continue the activity until each child has had a chance to come to the board and add a block.

- When you're through, close the file by tapping on the x in the upper right corner of the screen. Tap on *No* in the pop-up window.

SMART Tip

As your students become more skilled at patterning, make the activity more complicated by changing the orientation of a block or making blocks touch each other along a common edge. To change the orientation of a block, tap it. Then tap the green button at the top of the frame around the shape and drag it clockwise or counterclockwise until it looks the way you want.

Behind the Curtain

I found the images for this activity by typing "pattern blocks" in the search box of the *Gallery* tab. Then I clicked on the *Pictures* bar. I dragged each image I wanted onto the page and resized it. Then I selected each image on the page and activated the *Infinite Cloner* option in that image's drop-down menu. This feature allows each block to be repeatedly reused during the activity. With the *Text* tool, I created a text box and typed the activity title in the box. I found the cute musician figures in the *Gallery* too, by searching the term "band."

Days and Cents

Using coins to represent each day's date is a fast, simple way to sharpen your students' money skills as part of your daily calendar routine. For an extra challenge, ask your students to use money to show the number of days you've been in school. You'll have a roomful of bankers before you know it!

Days and Cents

Materials
- Plastic or real coins, a varied supply for each student

Before You Begin
Go to http://bit.ly/ZPNsvm (case sensitive) and download the SMART Notebook file for this activity. Distribute the coins to your students.

▶ **Check It Out!**
Go to **http://bit.ly/XLMGiY** (case sensitive) where I'll talk you through how I use this SMART Board activity with students.

Leading the Activity

◆ Open the SMART Notebook file to display the images of coins. Ask students to bring their coins and gather in front of the board. Explain that their job is to brainstorm and show all of the ways that today's date can be made using the coins.

◆ Give them an example, such as: "If today was the 12th, I could use a dime and two pennies to show the date." (Drag a dime and two pennies over to the open area of the page.) "I could also use two nickels and two pennies." (Drag those coins over as well.) "Does anyone have another idea about how I could use coins to show this date?" (After your class has done this activity a few times, you can skip the demonstration.)

◆ When you're finished demonstrating, tap the thumbnail in the *Page Sorter* tab, open the drop-down menu and choose the *Reset Page* option.

◆ Select a *Pen* tool and write the date you'll be working with in the upper right corner of the page.

- Ask for a volunteer to come to the board and show one way to make the date with coins. Ask the rest of the class to make a coin combination that shows the date too. Their coin combinations do not need to match the one at the board, as long as they equal the date in question.

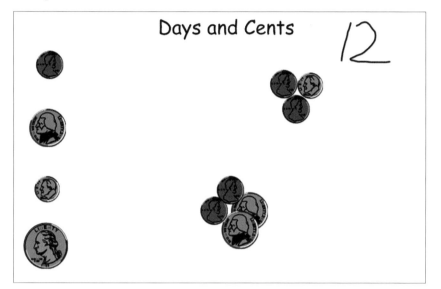

- Check in with the students working on the floor. Ask a few students to count aloud to confirm their combination is correct.

- When the student at the board is ready, check her work with the group. Make any adjustments necessary.

- If appropriate, ask for another volunteer to come to the board and show the date with a different combination of coins. Continue until there are no more possibilities.

- When you're through, close the file by tapping on the x in the upper right corner of the screen. Tap on *No* in the pop-up window.

Behind the Curtain

A nifty feature called *Infinite Cloner* is the secret to this page. I first used the *Text* tool to make a text box and type in the title. Then I searched for money images in the *Gallery* tab and dragged and dropped each coin image onto the page and sized it as needed. I selected each coin in turn and, using the drop-down menu, "turned on" the *Infinite Cloner* option.

SMART Tip

To quickly clear the page of coins, tap on the thumbnail image of the page in the *Page Sorter* tab, then tap on the gray menu arrow in the upper right corner. Choose the *Reset Page* option.

Main Street Matchup

Take a field trip to Main Street USA! The focus here is *goods* versus *services*—the difference between the two and which places in our towns and cities offer each. This is a nice introduction to a unit on your town or community. Your students will enjoy talking about the places they frequent in their neighborhoods. It's also a great opportunity to build some vocabulary!

Before You Begin

Go to http://bit.ly/16uGDm2 (case sensitive) and download the SMART Notebook file for this activity.

▶ Check It Out!

Go to **http://bit.ly/YuiZyx** (case sensitive) where I'll talk you through how I use this SMART Board activity with students.

SMART Tip

You can change the background color of any page with just a couple of clicks. Once you've opened a page, open the *Properties* tab. Click on the bar at the top of the tab that says *Fill Effects* and click the button below that—*Solid Fill*. Your color options will appear. Click on the one you like and watch your background come alive!

Leading the Activity

◆ Ask students to gather in front of the board. Spend a little time talking about goods and services if these are new concepts for your students. Explain that goods, in general, are items we take away from a business, such as groceries. Services are actions done to us or for us by a business, such as being given a haircut or having our trash picked up. In some cases, a business can provide both goods and services, and that provides food for discussion.

◆ Open the SMART Notebook file to display the Main Street scene. Explain to your students that their job will be to decide which of the places in this fictional town provide goods, which ones provide services, and which provide both. Point out the orange and yellow label buttons near the top of the page.

◆ Point out the images on the buildings; discuss how they provide a clue about what a business offers. Read the names if necessary. Ask for a volunteer to choose one business and drag the correct label to it. Repeat with other volunteers. Remind students that some of the businesses might need both labels, and ask them to tell you why in each case.

◆ After each student labels a particular spot on Main Street, talk about a similar business in your community. This is a terrific opportunity to plug in some vocabulary, such as *salon*, *groomer*, or *cinema*, so take advantage of it.

◆ When you're through, close the file by tapping on the x in the upper right corner of the screen. Tap on *No* in the pop-up window.

Behind the Curtain

Believe it or not, I made this fictional town simply by using the *Text* tool, the *Shapes* tool, and the *Color* tool. I combined and colored in shapes to make the buildings. I found the images (such as the dog and the egg) in the *Gallery* and dragged them onto the page. Then I resized them and placed them on the buildings.

Grammar Grab Bag

Students love a little mystery and the chance to work with a partner. This activity gives them both! The grab bag format makes practicing grammar more interesting, and the partner piece provides a low-risk environment for students. Who knew practicing grammar could be so much fun?

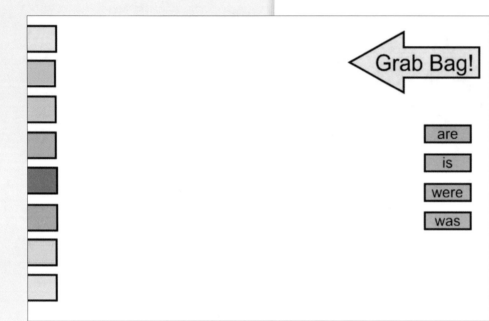

Materials
- Individual dry-erase boards
- Dry-erase markers

Before You Begin

Go to http://bit.ly/WfBJWS (case sensitive) and download the SMART Notebook file for this activity. Distribute the dry-erase boards and markers.

⏵ Check It Out!
Go to **http://bit.ly/Wq98wT** (case sensitive) where I'll talk you through how I use this SMART Board activity with students.

Leading the Activity

◆ Open the SMART Notebook file to display the color tabs and verbs. Assign students to groups of three, and ask them to bring their materials and gather in front of the board. Explain that their job will be to fill in the correct missing verb in a sentence. Point out the tabs at the left-hand side of the board, and explain that each one is a hidden sentence.

◆ Invite one group to the board and ask a group member to drag one of the colored tabs onto the board in full view. The group members will then read the sentence, decide which one of the words in the green rectangles will make sense to complete the sentence, and drag it into place. Ask the rest of the students to write their guesses on the dry-erase boards and hold them up when ready.

- Once the group at the board has chosen a word, read the sentence as a group and decide whether it makes sense. Remind students that, in some cases, more than one word will make sense.

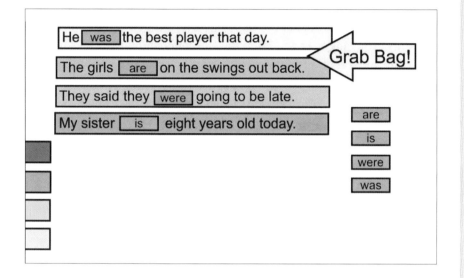

- If the sentence is complete, thank the group at the board and ask them to return to their spot near the board. If the sentence has not been completed correctly, enlist your students' help to fix it.

- Repeat, asking a new group of students to the board each time, until all of the colored tabs have been used.

- When you're through, close the file by tapping on the x in the upper right corner of the screen. Tap on *No* in the pop-up window.

Behind the Curtain

The *Text* tool, the *Shapes* tool, and the *Color* tool were part of my toolkit for this page. Once I'd made the rectangles and typed the sentences, I placed one sentence in each rectangle, and used the *Grouping* technique to combine them as a unit that I could drag across the page.

SMART Tip

Working with hidden sentences is cool, and it's so easy to do. Just click on the punctuation end of the rectangle and drag it to one side of the page, leaving just enough of the rectangle exposed so that it would be easy to pull into view. This trick often comes in handy when you're working with the SMART Board. Try it!

Place-Value Diamonds

A solid understanding of place value is an important foundation for achievement in math. This activity helps deepen it by asking students to think about the value of the digits involved, which is just what students are being asked to do in the Numbers and Operations in Base Ten section of the Common Core State Standards. This page has a reveal feature that appeals to students' love of mystery. In turn, you'll get a sense of what your students know and don't know about place value.

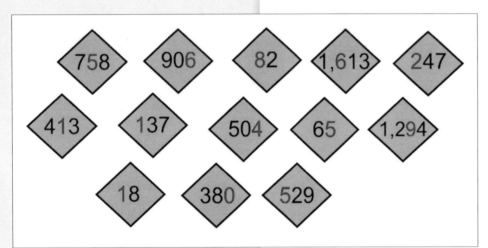

Materials
- Individual dry-erase boards
- Dry-erase markers

Before You Begin
Go to http://bit.ly/15OQ4Lz (case sensitive) and download the SMART Notebook file for this activity. Distribute the dry-erase boards and markers.

▶ Check It Out!
Go to **http://bit.ly/XzSGxe** (case sensitive) where I'll talk you through how I use this SMART Board activity with students.

Leading the Activity

- Open the SMART Notebook file to display the green diamonds with numbers inside. Ask students to bring their materials and gather in front of the board. Explain that they will be figuring out the *value* of the red digit in each number on the board. For example, in the number 529, 2 has a value of 20.

- Bring their attention to the first diamond, and ask for a volunteer to read the number aloud (or ask the whole class to read).

- Ask students to write the value of the red digit on their dry-erase boards and then display them.

- Reveal the value by dragging the diamond to the bottom of the page. The circle hidden beneath contains the correct answer.

- If your students were correct, you can ask a challenge question, such as what the values of the other digits are or what the number would be if you changed the red digit to a different numeral.

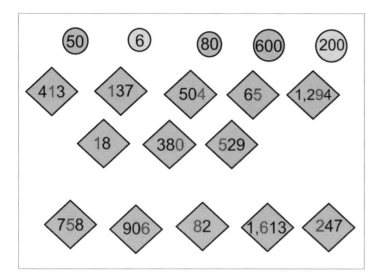

- If some students are incorrect, review the places of each number and what those mean. You may even choose to show them in expanded form by using a *Pen* tool to write directly on the SMART Board. (You can use the *Eraser* tool to wipe out notes like these before you move on.)

- Repeat the exercise with each number in turn.

- When you're through, close the file by tapping on the x in the upper right corner of the screen. Tap on *No* in the pop-up window.

Behind the Curtain

The *Shapes* tool allowed me to make this display of diamonds over hidden circles. I used the *Text* tool to write a number inside each shape. Next, I used a technique called *Grouping* to link together a shape and the number inside it. Then I used the *Order* technique to establish the two layers on the page: circles in back and diamonds in front.

SMART Tip

If your students need more visuals to help them understand this concept, base-ten block images are available in the *Gallery* tab. Add a blank page to your file by tapping the *Add Page* button in your toolbar. Then, open the *Gallery* tab and type "place value" in the search box at the top of the tab. Click on the blue *Related Folders* bar and open the *Place Value* folder. Double-click or drag and drop the blocks onto the blank page.

Add Page

How's Your Memory?

A solid sight-word vocabulary will help students become more fluent readers and writers. This activity gives you an opportunity to add another exposure to those important words in a rich and varied way. Students will like the larger-than-life board and the game-show atmosphere it creates.

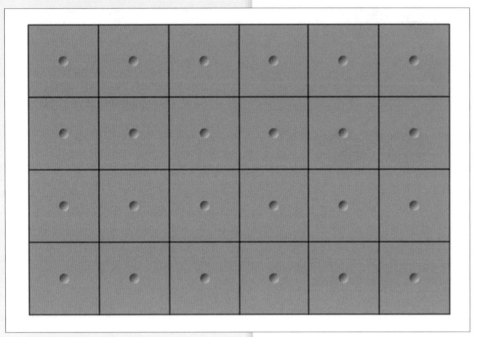

Before You Begin

Go to http://bit.ly/YtfhrW (case sensitive) and download the SMART Notebook file for this activity.

▶ Check It Out!

Go to **http://bit.ly/ZCMcZ2** (case sensitive) where I'll talk you through how I use this SMART Board activity with students.

Leading the Activity

◆ Open the SMART Notebook file to display the gray boxes. Ask students to gather in front of the board, and count off to create two teams. Ask them to sit in two single-file lines. Explain that there is a word hidden in each gray box and their job will be to find two words that match.

◆ Ask the first player on Team One to come to the board and tap two of the gray boxes to reveal two words. (Or invite students to come to the board in pairs; this can be a nice "lifeline" for emergent readers.)

◆ Ask the student to read each word aloud. If the words match, his team gets a point. If the words don't match, ask the student to tap the small gray triangles in the corners of the boxes to reapply the gray shading.

away	well	from	•	•	•
want	•	•	want	about	•
about	•	•	•	away	•
•	from	•	•	•	well

- Invite a Team Two player to come to the board and take a turn.

- Repeat, alternating between teams, until all of the matches have been made.

- When you're through, close the file by tapping on the x in the upper right corner of the screen. Tap on *No* in the pop-up window.

SMART Tip

To make sure certain words or images on a page can't be moved, simply "lock" them in place. That's what I did with this table to ensure a student wouldn't move a word by accident. Click and drag across the items you want to lock. Click on the arrow at the upper right corner of the frame. In the drop-down menu, choose the *Locking* option, then the *Lock In Place* option.

Behind the Curtain

The *Table* tool allowed me to create this nifty activity. After selecting the table size I wanted, I double-clicked in each cell and typed a word there. I used the *Color* tool to add the background color. To add the gray shading, I selected the entire table and then chose the *Add Table Shade* option from the drop-down menu.

Get On Board with Interactive Templates

Now that you've tried out some of the exciting SMART Board activities in Section 1, I'll bet you're ready for more. Here in Section 2 you'll find 14 creative activities, each highlighting a different interactive template found in SMART Notebook software.

I love working with the interactive templates, which are part of the *Lesson Activity Toolkit* in the SMART Notebook *Gallery*. These templates have "magical" features that allow students to take actions such as sorting items on the page, revealing hidden items, or rolling dice. Many interactive templates incorporate a self-checking feature, so you and your students can receive immediate feedback. Most of the templates are available in a variety of color schemes: brown, green, orange, purple, and teal. Choose the one you like best!

These activities are ready to use as is, but I encourage you to experiment. It's your choice. You can download the SMART Notebook file and simply follow the instructions in Leading the Activity. Or, you can follow the Now You're the Wizard instructions to create the magic yourself by customizing a template to generate your own unique version of an activity. Once you dive in, you'll quickly discover just how versatile these templates are and how easy they are to customize for almost any content and grade level. (You may need to employ a few SMART Notebook tools as you customize a template. For a quick tutorial on particular tools, flip to the Wizard's Guide beginning on page 160.) Check out Think of the Possibilities too, where I offer suggestions for adapting the activity for different grade levels or content areas.

As in Section 1, you'll find Web addresses for the downloadable files under Before You Begin, and Web addresses for two voice-over demonstrations for each activity under Check It Out!

Get your students involved too. You'll find they're eager to try customizing a template to share with the class. Let them get their creative juices flowing. Tasks such as creating questions and answers for a template really require a student to know the content, so it's a novel method for review and application. Ready to get on board? I guarantee you and your students will love these interactive activities!

Step to the next level as you discover the potential of SMART Notebook interactive templates.

SMART Tools and Techniques

Customizing the *Sentence Arrange* template

Reading Rearranged

You already know that practicing reading and listening comprehension is incredibly important. Using your SMART Board can add a touch of novelty to this task. This activity is designed to help students develop their sequencing and retelling skills. I've based the instructions here on the book *The Dot* by Peter Reynolds, but you can replicate it with almost anything you and your students read.

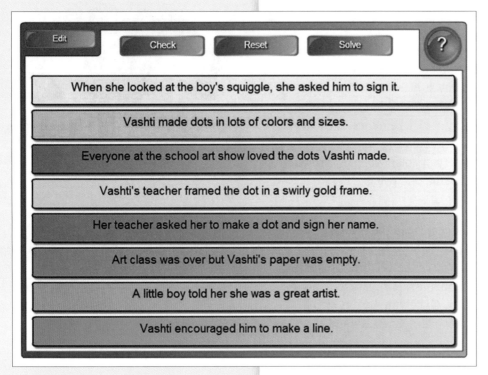

| Edit | Check | Reset | Solve | ? |

When she looked at the boy's squiggle, she asked him to sign it.

Vashti made dots in lots of colors and sizes.

Everyone at the school art show loved the dots Vashti made.

Vashti's teacher framed the dot in a swirly gold frame.

Her teacher asked her to make a dot and sign her name.

Art class was over but Vashti's paper was empty.

A little boy told her she was a great artist.

Vashti encouraged him to make a line.

Materials
- Photocopies of the sentences on the activity page, 1 for each student
- Scissors
- A copy of *The Dot* by Peter Reynolds

Before You Begin

Go to http://bit.ly/XzDosm (case sensitive) and download the SMART Notebook file for this activity. Distribute the photocopies and scissors, and ask your students to cut out each sentence as a separate strip.

▶ Check It Out!

Go to **http://bit.ly/16uX5CJ** (case sensitive) where I'll talk you through how to lead this activity.

SMART Tip

After you've used this as a whole-class activity, your students can redo it as a center or anchor activity. If you want a record of their work, ask them to use a *Pen* tool to write their name on the page and show them how to print their product by using the *Print* tool in the toolbar.

Leading the Activity

◆ Read *The Dot* aloud to your students. Open the SMART Notebook file to display the sentences. Ask your students to bring their materials and gather in front of the board.

◆ Explain that the sentences on the SMART Board retell the story of *The Dot,* but they are not in the correct order. Tell students that their job will be to put the events of the story in order, dragging and dropping sentences up or down on the board. The SMART Board is so smart that it will automatically make room for the sentences as they move! Read each sentence aloud to your students.

◆ Ask your students for some suggestion about what the first important event in the story was. Help them to narrow down their ideas to reflect the sentence that should come first.

◆ Invite a volunteer to come to the board to find that sentence and drag it to its appropriate place at the top of the page. Ask the rest of the class to find that sentence among their strips of paper and lay it on the floor.

◆ Continue discussing ideas and inviting volunteers to the board until your students feel that all the sentences are arranged in the right order. (Students working on the floor will continue laying out strips in sequence.) To check their work, tap the *Check* button at the top of the page. A green check mark means that a sentence is in the correct spot; a red x signals incorrect placement.

◆ If there are errors, ask students to revise the sequence.

◆ Once the sentences are 100 percent correct, close the file by tapping on the x in the upper right corner of the screen. Tap on *No* in the pop-up window. (The next time you open the file, the sentences will be scrambled again.)

Now You're the Wizard

In the *Gallery* tab, click on *Lesson Activity Toolkit*. Click on the blue bar titled *Interactive and Multimedia*. Scroll down to find one of the *Sentence Arrange* templates. Double-click or drag and drop it onto your page. Click on the *Edit* button at the top left of the page, and the screen will change. Now you click on each sentence bar in turn and type in your text.

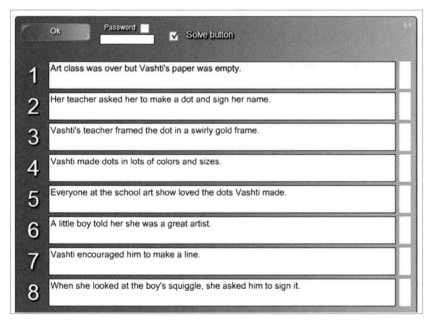

You will not see a cursor appear in the bars, which makes editing a little different until you get used to it. If you want to erase a chunk of text or a whole sentence, click and highlight the words you'd like to delete, and then hit the *Backspace* key on your keyboard. It's pretty similar to word processing, so you can do it! Be sure to type the sentences in correct sequential order. When you're finished, click on the *Ok* button and then name and save the file.

Think of the Possibilities

You can use this activity with a story from your reading series, a chapter book (make a new page for each chapter), a nonfiction book, or a textbook chapter. Or branch out from reading and try it as a sequencing activity for relating the order of the life cycle of a frog or other organism or the order of important historic events.

▶ Check It Out!
Go to **http://bit.ly/YtCSbW** (case sensitive) where I'll explain how to work with the *Sentence Arrange* template.

SMART Tip

This template has a password option in the edit screen. You can set a password if you want to ensure that your content doesn't get changed without your permission.

SMART Tools and Techniques

Customizing the *Note Reveal* template

Daily Message

A written greeting from you is a nice way to start your students' day. When that greeting is written on your SMART Board, it also provides some valuable opportunities for interactive review. The complexity of the sentences can grow with your students and so can the amount they contribute to the message each week or month. Make the message subject specific to tickle their imaginations before starting a new science or social studies unit.

Before you Begin

Go to http://bit.ly/Wq1VwP (case sensitive) and download the SMART Notebook file for this activity.

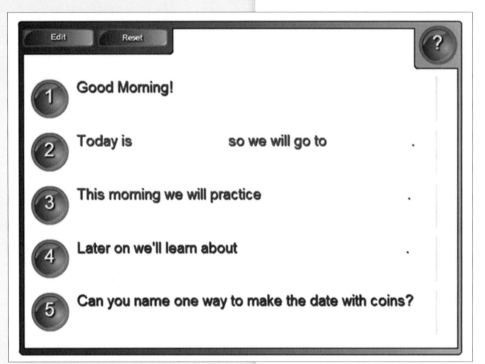

▶ Check It Out!

Go to **http://bit.ly/13YrLNg** (case sensitive) where I'll talk you through how to lead this activity.

Leading the Activity

◆ Open the SMART Notebook file to display the "invisible" message. Ask students to join you on the floor in front of the board. Explain that their job will be to help you read the message and figure out what words are missing. (After you've done this activity a few times, you can skip the directions.)

◆ Reveal the entire message by tapping each number on the screen in turn. Read the entire message to your students, saying "blank" for each blank space. Tap the *Reset* button in the upper left corner of the template.

◆ Press the number 1 and the number 2 to reveal the first two lines of text. Reread until you come to the first blank. Ask a few students to make a guess about the word they think is missing, then invite one volunteer to come to the board and use a *Pen* tool to write the missing word he believes fits. Help with spelling as necessary.

- Reread from the beginning until you come to the next blank and repeat the process. If you wish, students can chime in on the rereading each time to build some fluency.

- When you're ready to reveal the next line of text, tap the *Select* button to deactivate the *Pen* tool. Continue the activity, adding one line at a time, until you've revealed the entire message.

- Once all of the blanks have been filled in, read it one more time through with your students.

- When you're through, close the file by tapping on the x in the upper right corner of the screen. Tap on *No* in the pop-up window.

Now You're the Wizard

In the *Gallery* tab, click on *Lesson Activity Toolkit.* Click on the blue bar titled *Interactive and Multimedia.* Scroll down to find one of the *Note Reveal* templates. Double-click or drag and drop the template onto your SMART Notebook page. Click the *Edit* button and type in your

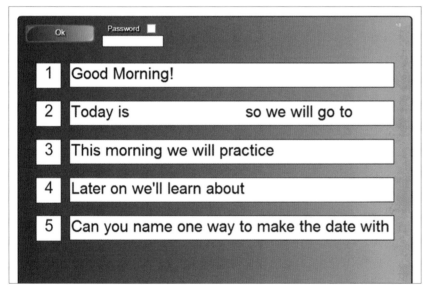

content. Note that in the template, the words will appear as black type on your screen. The template magically converts the type into different colors when it displays the finished page. Click the *Ok* button and name and save the file.

Think of the Possibilities

To mix things up a bit, try writing an entire message without any blank spaces. Instead, include spelling, grammar, or punctuation errors that your students would recognize, and ask volunteers to find and fix the mistakes. Your errors could reflect your weekly spelling list, a word family or vowel pattern you've studied, or sight or vocabulary words that your students need to know.

For a social studies lesson, use this template to construct an "on this day in history . . ." message, where you can include famous birthdays or important historic events.

⮑ Check It Out!

Go to **http://bit.ly/13Vuerw** (case sensitive) where I'll explain how to work with the *Note Reveal* template.

SMART Tip

For this activity, you'll need to create blanks where the students will fill in words. There are two ways to accomplish that: Simply hit the *Space* bar on your keyboard about 10 times (which is what I did), or insert a line using the *Lines* tool.

Lines

SMART Tools and Techniques

Customizing the *Random Word Chooser* template

Show Me

While nouns, verbs, and adjectives are the main characters here, your students will also begin to acquire some sophisticated vocabulary as you move through this lesson. So if you're looking for another way to practice those general academic words the Common Core State Standards talk about, this is it! The automaticity of this activity makes it appealing to everyone. This template has versatility too: Practice math facts and more!

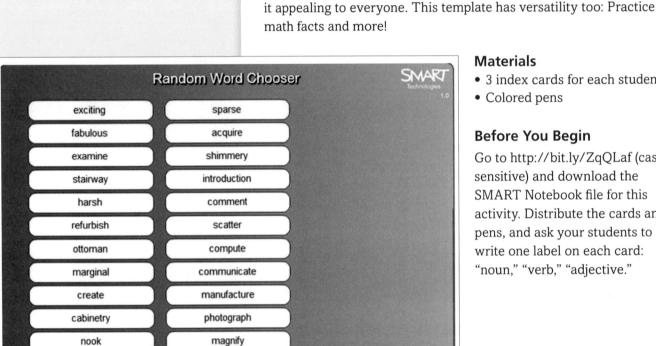

Materials

- 3 index cards for each student
- Colored pens

Before You Begin

Go to http://bit.ly/ZqQLaf (case sensitive) and download the SMART Notebook file for this activity. Distribute the cards and pens, and ask your students to write one label on each card: "noun," "verb," "adjective."

◗ Check It Out!

Go to **http://bit.ly/Z6Vezw** (case sensitive) where I'll talk you through how to lead this activity.

Leading the Activity

◆ Open the SMART Notebook file to display the set of words. Ask students to bring their materials and gather in front of the board. Explain that their job will be to identify the part of speech for each word the *Random Word Chooser* selects. Then, at your signal, they will hold up the correct card to identify the part of speech.

◆ To begin, press the *Select* button at the bottom of the page. The software will cycle through a few words and then stop on one and make it slightly larger. Read the word to your students if necessary and then say: "Three, two, one . . . show me!"

◆ Check your students' selections. If anyone has made the wrong selection, simply state which card should be held up and why. For example: "I should see the card that says 'noun' because the word *stairway* is a noun. It's a thing."

- If all your students have the correct answer, congratulate them! You might choose to say something like: "Great! Everyone is showing me their noun card. That's right because nouns are people, places, and things, and a stairway is a thing."

- Press the *Select* button again and repeat the process as many times as you wish.

- When you're through, close the file by tapping on the x in the upper right corner of the screen. Tap on *No* in the pop-up window.

Now You're the Wizard

In the *Gallery* tab, click on *Lesson Activity Toolkit*. Click on the blue bar titled *Interactive and Multimedia*. Scroll down to find the *Random Word Chooser* template (there's only one). Double-click or drag and drop the template onto your SMART Notebook page. Your first step is to

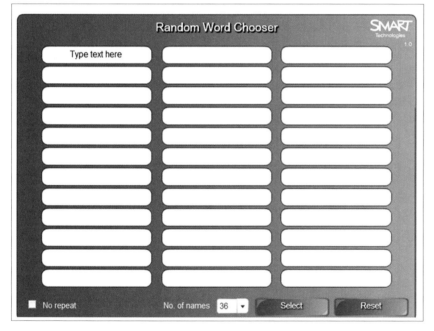

use the drop-down menu at the bottom of the template to choose the number of words you want to display—36 is the maximum. Then simply click on each box in turn and type in a word or math expression. Once you've filled in all the boxes, name and save the file.

Think of the Possibilities

If the words I've chosen are too complex for your students, set up the template with simpler words. Sight words work well here too: Skip the index cards, and make your signal, "Three, two, one . . . say it!" Your students can call out the word as a group.

No need to restrict the activity to words, either. Set up the template with math expressions in each box, and ask your students to call out the solution. What a great way to practice math facts!

▶ Check It Out!

Go to **http://bit.ly/WghM29** (case sensitive) where I'll explain how to work with the *Random Word Chooser* template.

SMART Tip

This template also has an image version. It's called *Random Image Chooser*. You can find an activity that uses that version on page 52. It's called Blenders.

SMART Tools and Techniques

Customizing the *Random Image Chooser* template

Blenders

Phonics requires a lot of practice, especially when you go beyond initial consonants. The lively nature of this template promises to make that practice engaging. The example below focuses on consonant blends and students' ability to encode them. The image-based format of this activity makes it an excellent fit for other letter or sound activities as well. The best part is that students don't need to be able to read to interact with it!

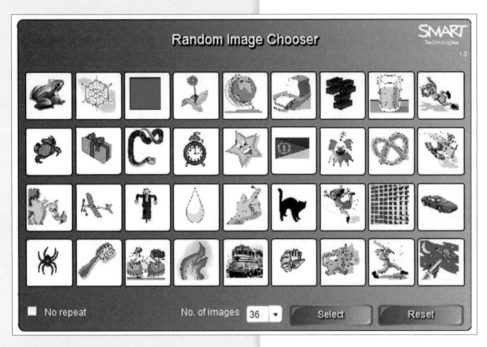

Materials

- Individual dry-erase boards
- Dry-erase markers

Before You Begin

Go to http://bit.ly/10M9YEg (case sensitive) and download the SMART Notebook file for this activity. Distribute the dry-erase boards and markers.

▶ Check It Out!

Go to **http://bit.ly/10SGgkJ** (case sensitive) where I'll talk you through how to lead this activity.

Leading the Activity

- ◆ Open the SMART Notebook file to display the graphic chart. Ask students to bring their materials and join you in front of the board. Explain that their job will be to listen for the consonant blend they hear at the beginning of the name of the image selected and then write it on their dry-erase boards.

- ◆ Press the *Select* button and wait for the software to select an image. Ask students to think about what consonant blend is at the beginning of the word, write it on their boards, and hold up the boards for you to see.

- ◆ When students are ready, check their boards and correct any errors. If you wish, you can also ask students to name other words that begin with the same consonant blend.

- Repeat the process as many times as you wish.

- When you're through, close the file by tapping on the x in the upper right corner of the screen. Tap on *No* in the pop-up window.

Now You're the Wizard

In the *Gallery* tab, click on *Lesson Activity Toolkit.* Click on the blue bar titled *Interactive and Multimedia.* Scroll down to the *Random Image Chooser* template (there's only one of these). Double-click or drag and drop the template onto your SMART Notebook page. Choose

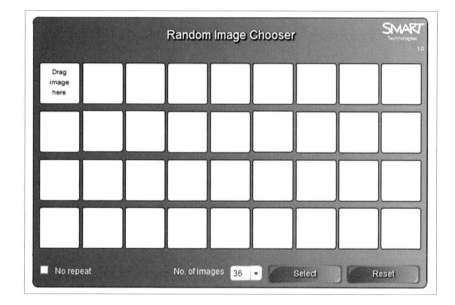

the number of images you want by using the drop-down menu at the bottom of the template. To add images, click on *Gallery Essentials* in the *Gallery* tab and then the blue bar titled *Pictures.* Then drag and drop one image into each square—the template will size them for you! When you're done, click the x in the upper right corner of the page and name and save the file.

Think of the Possibilities

Use your imagination! Set up a chart with pictures of food items, and ask students to tell you whether a food is a healthy or unhealthy choice. For a science activity, ask students to state whether an image is of a living thing or a nonliving thing. For a social studies activity, set up the chart with historic figures or landmarks, and simply ask students to identify the image selected. Do the same thing with shapes for a math activity.

SMART Tip

Random selection is a cool feature of this template, but keep in mind that the template may select the same image more than once. If you don't want that to happen, simply check the **No repeat** box at the bottom left of the screen.

▶ Check It Out!
Go to **http://bit.ly/WghR6e** (case sensitive) where I'll explain how to work with the *Random Image Chooser* template.

SMART Tools and Techniques

Customizing the *Pairs* template

Buddy Up

Challenge your students' memory power and build their phonics skills in this game of rhyming pairs. The fast-moving play will keep everyone involved. The beauty of this memory-game format is that it can be adapted to most subject areas and the words you choose can be more or less complicated. In addition, the skills featured here tie in nicely with the Reading Foundational Skills section of the Common Core State Standards. You can even program this template with images or numbers rather than words. So get those thinking caps on!

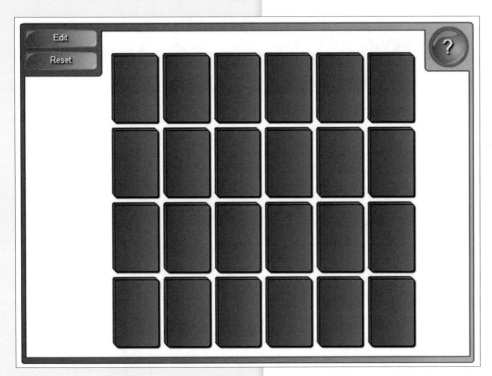

Before You Begin

Go to http://bit.ly/XazgsT (case sensitive) and download the SMART Notebook file for this activity.

▶ Check It Out!

Go to **http://bit.ly/ZCMwXG** (case sensitive) where I'll talk you through how to lead this activity.

Leading the Activity

◆ Open the SMART Notebook file to display the Buddy Up playing board. Divide students into two groups, and ask them to sit or stand in line in front of the board.

◆ Explain that a word is hidden behind each purple card, and their job will be to work in pairs to find a pair of rhyming words.

◆ Ask the first student in each line to come to the board. One member of this pair will tap a card on the board. The card will flip over to reveal the word. The other member of the pair will tap a different card to reveal a second word at the same time. If the two words rhyme, the match is correct, and the cards will disappear. If the word pair is not a match, the cards will flip back over.

- Continue inviting pairs of students to the board in turn. As each correct pair is found, challenge your students to brainstorm other words that would rhyme with the pair or fit into its word family.

- Play continues until time runs out or all cards have been matched.

- When you're through, close the file by tapping on the x in the upper right corner of the screen. Tap on *No* in the pop-up window.

Now You're the Wizard

In the *Gallery* tab, click on *Lesson Activity Toolkit*. Click on the blue bar titled *Interactive and Multimedia*. Scroll down to find one of the *Pairs* templates. Double-click or drag and drop the template onto your SMART Notebook page. Click on the *Edit* button. Now you can decide how many pairs you want to include and add content to each card.

Click on the card you want to start with and type a word or drag and drop an image. Continue with the other cards. Whatever you type or place on card number 1, be sure to type or place the matching content on the other card numbered 1. To edit any text, click and highlight it, then edit as you would if you were word processing. Once you've finished, click the *Ok* button. Name and save the file.

Think of the Possibilities

A memory-game format can be adapted to practice almost any skill with any age group. Traditional matches can consist of identical images, letters, words, or numbers.

Nontraditional matches might consist of a number and a mathematical expression that equals that number, a word and its part of speech or definition, two homonyms, two synonyms, two antonyms, a story element and a text detail from the story, or even two objects that belong to the same category. Be creative!

SMART Tip

In this template, you have the option of numbering the tiles. When you are using many pairs, numbered tiles may help students keep track of the location of certain words more readily. If students are a little more advanced in skill, they might like the challenge of unnumbered tiles. You can change this at any time by tapping the *Edit* button and checking or unchecking *Show tile numbers*.

▶ Check It Out!
Go to **http://bit.ly/YtDfTY** (case sensitive) where I'll explain how to work with the *Pairs* template.

SMART Tools and Techniques

Customizing the *Keyword Match* template

What Time Do You Have?

Telling time is more than just being able to read a clock. It also encompasses understanding the many ways to state the time. This activity asks kids to match digital times with their wordy counterparts and to show the time on an analog clock. Good news: It's a perfect match to some of the Measurement and Data expectations in the Common Core State Standards. The matchup template used in this activity presents almost endless possibilities!

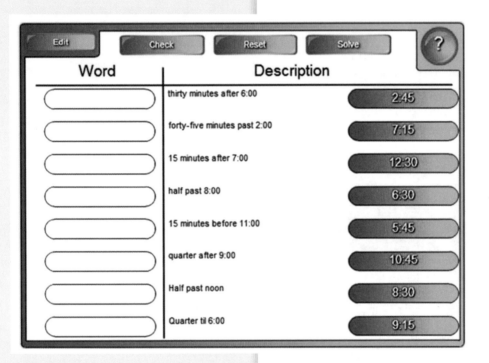

Materials
• Laminated blank clock faces
• Dry-erase markers

Before You Begin
Go to http://bit.ly/151Su7z (case sensitive) and download the SMART Notebook file for this activity. Distribute the clock faces and markers.

▶ Check It Out!
Go to **http://bit.ly/WK7A3b** (case sensitive) where I'll talk you through how to lead this activity.

Leading the Activity

♦ Open the SMART Notebook file to display the keyword matching chart. Ask students to bring their materials and join you in front of the SMART Board. Explain that their job will be to show the time displayed digitally on the screen in analog format using their markers and clock faces.

♦ Ask a volunteer to come to the board and choose one of the times displayed digitally on the right side of the page and drag it across to the correct descriptive phrase.

♦ While the student at the board makes his decision, the rest of the class can work with their markers and clock faces. You might also pose other time-making tasks to the rest of the class, such as asking them to show 20 minutes past 7 o'clock on their clock faces.

♦ Check students' work and make any corrections necessary.

♦ Choose another volunteer and repeat the process. Once all the times have been placed, tap the *Check* button at the top of the page so that your students can see how well they did. The times that have green check marks next to them are in the correct spot and the ones with a red x are not. Ask your students to help you get everything in the correct spot.

♦ When you're through, close the file by tapping on the x in the upper right corner of the screen. Tap on *No* in the pop-up window.

Now You're the Wizard

In the *Gallery* tab, click on *Lesson Activity Toolkit*. Click on the blue bar titled *Interactive and Multimedia*. Scroll down to find one of the *Keyword Match* templates. Double-click or drag and drop the template onto your SMART Notebook page. Click the *Edit* button and type in your keywords and descriptions. Click on *Ok* and name and save the file.

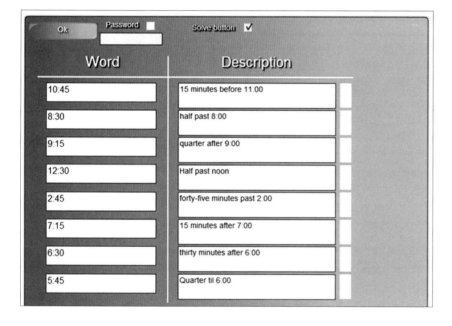

If you teach social studies, consider matching quotes to famous people or dates to important events. For a science activity, ask students to match animal mothers and babies, animals and habitats, or items and states of matter.

Matching also works well for math vocabulary and definitions or math expressions and solutions.

▶ Check It Out!
Go to **http://bit.ly/Zr4Swe** (case sensitive) where I'll explain how to work with the *Keyword Match* template.

SMART Tip
Many SMART Notebook templates include a *Solve* button at the top of the page. Use this if your students are stuck and can't seem to get things just right. Tapping that button will place everything in the correct place or order.

SMART Tools and Techniques

Customizing the *Multiple Choice* template

Number-Story Game Show

Play money for prizes lends extra fun to this flexible multiple-choice-format activity. As each child works on her own to figure out and display her "final answer" to single and multistep word problems, she is also developing what the Common Core State Standards call knowledge of Operations and Algebraic Thinking. Who knew? You can adapt this activity to almost any content you teach; it's a lively way to review information!

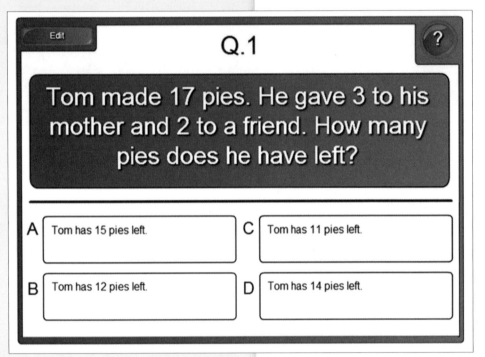

Materials

- Individual dry-erase boards
- Dry-erase markers
- A stopwatch (or clock with a second hand)

Before You Begin

Go to http://bit.ly/15OTM82 (case sensitive) and download the SMART Notebook file for this activity. Distribute the dry-erase boards and markers.

⊙ Check It Out!

Go to **http://bit.ly/Wqa58y** (case sensitive) where I'll talk you through how to lead this activity.

Leading the Activity

♦ Open the SMART Notebook file that contains this page and display it on your board. Ask students to bring their materials and gather in front of the board. Explain that this lesson is like a game show. They will have a given amount of time to solve a word problem. Prizes are offered for correct answers!

♦ Read the first problem to your students. Allow them an appropriate amount of time to solve it; then ask them to show you their final answer by holding up their dry-erase boards.

♦ Tap the answer that is correct, and have students compare their answer to the one you tapped on the board. Award play money as a prize to those with the correct answer.

- To extend the learning, ask one or two of the students who got the correct answer to explain how they solved the problem.

- Tap the *Next* button at the top of the page to reveal the next number story, and repeat the process for the remaining three stories.

- When you're through, close the file by tapping on the x in the upper right corner of the screen. Tap on *No* in the pop-up window.

Now You're the Wizard

In the *Gallery* tab, click on *Lesson Activity Toolkit*. Click on the blue bar titled *Interactive and Multimedia*. Scroll down to find one of the *Multiple Choice* templates. Double-click or drag and drop the template onto your SMART Notebook page. Click the *Edit* button and type in your

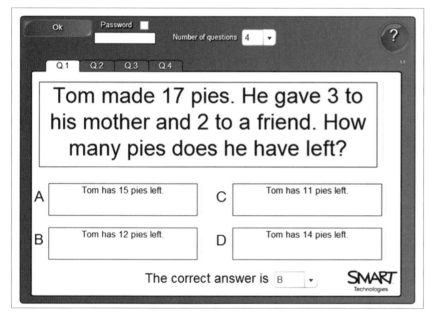

questions and answers. Be sure to select A, B, C, or D from the *The correct answer is* menu at the bottom of the template. This tells the software which answer should be given the green check mark. This is especially important if you envision your students using this activity independently during a center or anchor activity time. When you're done, click the *Ok* button, then name and save the file.

▶ Check It Out!
Go to **http://bit.ly/13YwtdO** (case sensitive) where I'll explain how to work with the *Multiple Choice* template.

SMART Tip

If you want to do more than four number stories, no worries! When you edit the template, use the drop-down menu at the top

of the page to choose any number of questions up to 10. To go beyond 10, click on the *Add Page* tool to add another page to your file and drag and drop an additional template onto it.

Think of the Possibilities

With this template, any content you can put into question format will work! Add questions about the events in a book to test student comprehension or fill in vocabulary words and their definitions. You can also ask questions such as "Which sentence doesn't make sense?" and then have students choose A, B, C, or D accordingly.

For a more challenging exercise, ask your students to create a set of four multiple-choice questions focusing on a particular area of study or topic.

SMART Tools and Techniques

Customizing the *Image Select* template

Our Nation's Symbols

Our national historic symbols and landmarks and significant historic figures are images students should be able to recognize. This fast-moving activity combines photos and portraits with words to reinforce your students' memories of these important images. This template also serves well for memory practice of shapes and numbers.

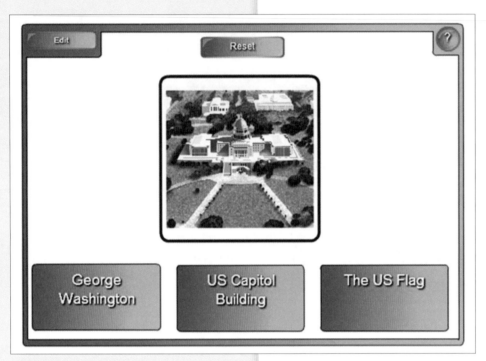

Materials
- Index cards, 3 for each student
- Markers, 1 for each student

Before You Begin

Go to http://bit.ly/XzOUny (case sensitive) and download the SMART Notebook file for this activity. Distribute the cards and ask students to label each card with one letter: A, B, C.

▶ **Check It Out!**
Go to **http://bit.ly/Z1Vehj** (case sensitive) where I'll talk you through how to lead this activity.

Leading the Activity

◆ Ask students to bring their index cards and gather in front of the board. Tell students to lay out the index cards on the floor. Explain that their job will be to name the landmark, symbol, or person that appears on the screen. They will be able to choose from three possible answers (A, B, or C) and will indicate their response by holding up the corresponding index card when you give them a signal.

◆ Open the SMART Notebook file to display the flashing slide show of images. Tap on the image box and the slide show will freeze, displaying just one picture. Three possible labels for the picture will appear at the bottom of the template. Explain that A stands for the image on the left, B for the image in the middle, and C for the image on the right. Count "Three, two, one . . . name that symbol."

◆ Review the cards in view, and tap on the answer that most of your students chose. If they are correct, a green check mark will appear and the images will start cycling again. If they are incorrect, a red x will appear on the wrong answer and then fade away, allowing students to make another choice.

◆ Repeat the process for as many rounds as you wish.

◆ When you're through, close the file by tapping on the x in the upper right corner of the screen. Tap on *No* in the pop-up window.

Now You're the Wizard

In the *Gallery* tab, click on *Lesson Activity Toolkit*. Click on the blue bar titled *Interactive and Multimedia*. Scroll down to find one of the *Image Select* templates. Double-click or drag and drop the template onto your SMART Notebook page. Click the *Edit* button and drag and drop images from the *Gallery* onto the page. Type the label for each one.

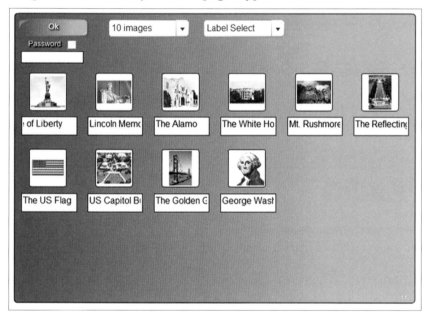

You can also choose how many images you want in the mix by using the drop-down menu at the top of the template. Once you've filled in the number of images you want, click *Ok* and name and save the page.

▶ Check It Out!
Go to **http://bit.ly/Z1YCJ0** (case sensitive) where I'll explain how to work with the *Image Select* template.

SMART Tip

If you want, students can label the images in this activity themselves instead of selecting a prewritten label. When you are in the *Edit* screen, choose *Handwriting* instead of *Label Select* from the drop-down menu at the top of the template.

Think of the Possibilities

This template doesn't always have to be used for lessons with such weighty content. Try using it to help your students learn to recognize shapes, continents, states, or everyday items such as kitchen tools or fruits and vegetables.

SMART Tools and Techniques

Customizing the *Word Guess* template

Sounds the Same

Homonyms can be tricky for almost anyone, especially for those just learning to read and write or for English language learners. This activity adds a splash of fun to studying those sticky word pairs with a "tomato splat" theme your students will love. You can use this template to review spelling or vocabulary words, or even math, science, and social studies content.

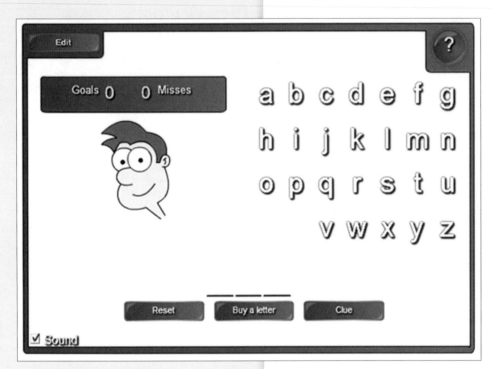

Before You Begin

Go to http://bit.ly/ZCKk2f (case sensitive) and download the SMART Notebook file for this activity.

▶ Check It Out!

Go to **http://bit.ly/13Vqczh** (case sensitive) where I'll talk you through how to lead this activity.

SMART Tip

If your students are old enough, they can create their own pages for class use. Creating an activity like this gives students additional exposure to the content and requires them to think even more deeply to develop appropriate clues for their classmates.

Leading the Activity

◆ Open the SMART Notebook file to display the Word Guess scoreboard. Ask students to gather in front of the board. Explain that their job will be to guess *and* spell the homonym for the word displayed in the clue.

◆ Ask for a volunteer to run the board for the first round. Tell the volunteer to tap the *Clue* button at the bottom right of the screen and read the clue to the rest of the group (with help if necessary).

◆ Point out the blanks that appear on the screen. These represent the letters of the mystery homonym.

◆ Ask the other children to stand up when they think they know what the homonym is. Next ask for volunteers, one at a time, to come to the board and tap a letter they think is in the mystery homonym. If they guess correctly, the letter will appear in the correct blank spot, a tomato will splat on the man's face, and their answer will be recorded as a Goal. If they guess incorrectly, the tomato will miss the man, and their answer will be counted as a Miss.

- Once the mystery homonym is spelled out correctly, your SMART Board will congratulate you and your students.

- Tap the *Next* button on the bottom of the page to reveal the next word or clue and continue through the bank of words you've programmed.

- When you're through, close the file by tapping on the x in the upper right corner of the screen. Tap on *No* in the pop-up window.

Now You're the Wizard

In the *Gallery* tab, click on *Lesson Activity Toolkit.* Click on the blue bar titled *Interactive and Multimedia.* Scroll down to find one of the *Word Guess* templates. Double-click or drag and drop the template onto your SMART Notebook page. Click the *Edit* button and type your mystery homonyms or other content in the left-hand column and the corresponding clues in the right-hand column. If you're preparing a math

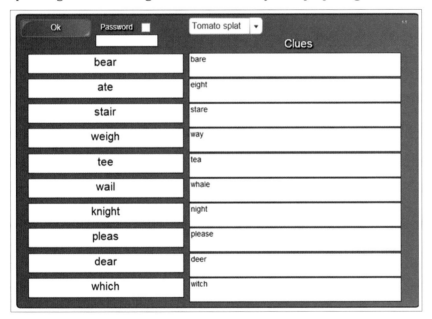

activity, keep in mind that you can use numerals for your clues, but the content in the left-hand column must be spelled out—numerals won't work. When you're finished, click the *Ok* button. Name and save the file.

Think of the Possibilities

Customize this template for reviewing each week's spelling words or definitions of the vocabulary words from a story or a textbook chapter. Opposites and synonyms work well for this activity too.

Even math vocabulary words fit here. Use numerals as the clue and ask students to spell the number word. Math expressions as clues would require students to figure out the solution and spell the answers.

▶ Check It Out!

Go to **http://bit.ly/Z1YE3s** (case sensitive) where I'll explain how to work with the *Word Guess* template.

SMART Tip

Tomato splat is just one of three possible themes for this activity. On the *Edit* screen for this template, you can click on the drop-down menu to choose a soccer or basketball theme instead. Remember to click on the *Ok* button too!

SMART Tools and Techniques

Customizing the *Category Sort* template

Match My Expression

A math lesson that stimulates students to think about multiple approaches to solving math expressions is always a good idea—and this activity does just that! Students will love the twist on traditional math facts, and you'll love the extra practice they'll get. This three-way sorting format is also a good catalyst for vocabulary building.

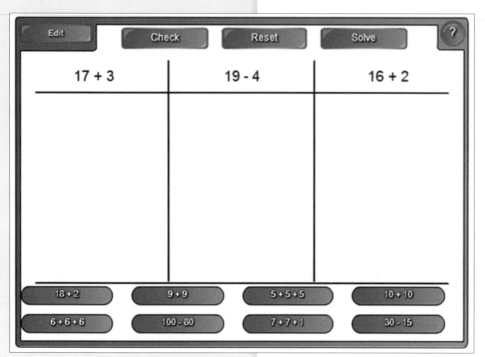

Materials

- Paper copies of a hundred square, 1 for each student

Before You Begin

Go to http://bit.ly/XazRuQ (case sensitive) and download the SMART Notebook file for this activity. Distribute the hundred squares.

▶ Check It Out!

Go to **http://bit.ly/13Vqm9N** (case sensitive) where I'll talk you through how to lead this activity.

Leading the Activity

◆ Open the SMART Notebook file to display the three-column format and math expressions. Ask students to bring their hundred squares and join you on the floor in front of the board. Explain that they will be solving math expressions and sorting those expressions according to their answers. The trick is that they will be grouping the expressions with others that are equivalent.

◆ Ask for a volunteer to come to the board and drag and drop one of the expressions into the appropriate column. (The expression at the top of the column has the same solution as the expression they are moving.)

◆ Direct the rest of the class to use their hundred squares to figure out where the expressions go.

◆ Continue encouraging students to solve the expressions remaining at the bottom of the page and asking for volunteers to move an expression on the board into one of the columns.

- Once all of the expressions have been placed in a column on the board, tap the *Check* button at the top of the page. A green check mark indicates a correct answer; a red x indicates a wrong answer.

- Enlist your students' help to place any incorrect items in their appropriate spots.

- When you're through, close the file by tapping on the x in the upper right corner of the screen. Tap on *No* in the pop-up window.

Now You're the Wizard

In the *Gallery* tab, click on *Lesson Activity Toolkit*. Click on the blue bar titled *Interactive and Multimedia*. Scroll down to find one of the *Category Sort* templates. Double-click or drag and drop the template onto your SMART Notebook page. Click the *Edit* button. To start, decide whether you want to create a two- or three-column sorting

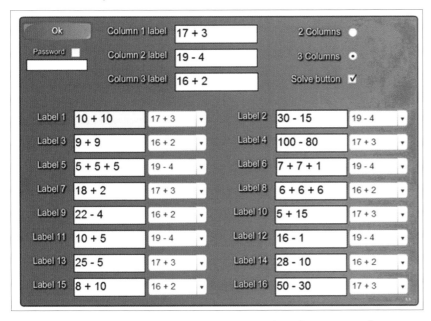

activity. Then type in content that is appropriate for your students. When you're finished, click the *Ok* button. Name and save the file.

Think of the Possibilities

Instead of using this template for math practice, set it up with three words that your students overuse in writing as column headers. For the items to be dragged and dropped, fill in synonyms for the column heading words. You might also choose to have students sort words by parts of speech or number of syllables.

▶ Check It Out!

Go to **http://bit.ly/WgiJHZ** (case sensitive) where I'll explain how to work with the *Category Sort* template.

SMART Tip

Remember: When you're creating a three-column page, each time you add content to the template in edit mode, click on the drop-down menu for that item and indicate which column it belongs in.

SMART Tools and Techniques

Customizing the *Vortex Sort* template

The Long and the Short of It

Recognizing vowel sounds is an important part of our students' reading and writing efforts. This sorting activity will focus their attention on listening for the long and the short sound of /a/. The spinning vortices on this template and its self-checking features will make it a favorite with your students for sure. The best part is that once you know how to use this template, the sorting possibilities in any content area are almost endless!

Sort It Out

Edit   Reset   ?

Long a   Short a

day   ape   late   came

can   at   tap   ant

Before You Begin

Go to http://bit.ly/ZqUMeP (case sensitive) and download the SMART Notebook file for this activity.

▶ Check It Out!

Go to **http://bit.ly/ZqYmpo** (case sensitive) where I'll talk you through how to lead this activity.

Leading the Activity

◆ Open the SMART Notebook file that contains this page and display it on your board. Ask students to gather in front of the board. Explain that their job will be to separate words that have the long sound of /a/ from those with the short sound and place them in the correct vortex. Point out the labels on the vortices and read them aloud if necessary.

◆ Ask for a volunteer to come to the SMART board and drag one word onto the correct vortex and wait for the results. If the vortex absorbs the word, the student has guessed the vowel sound correctly and congratulations are in order! If the vortex throws the word back out, the word does not have that vowel sound. Isolate the vowel sound aloud for your students so that they can hear it clearly and then place it in the correct vortex.

- Continue with other volunteers and the remaining words until each one has been placed properly.
- When you're through, close the file by tapping on the x in the upper right corner of the screen. Tap on *No* in the pop-up window.

Now You're the Wizard

In the *Gallery* tab, click on *Lesson Activity Toolkit*. Click on the blue bar titled *Interactive and Multimedia*. Scroll down to find one of the *Vortex Sort* templates. Double-click or drag and drop the template onto your page. Click on the *Edit* button in the upper left corner of the page.

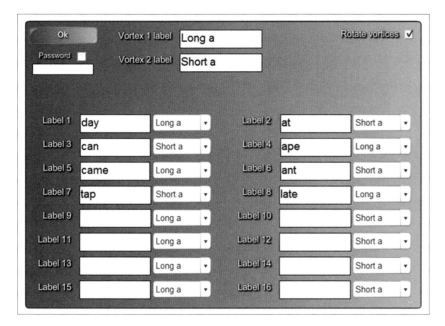

Type the titles of your vortices at the top of the page. Then type a word in each label slot and choose the correct vortex from the drop-down menu. Be sure to type the words in random order so they show up that way when you reset the template. Once your content is complete, click the *Ok* button in the upper left corner of the page. Name and save the file.

▶ **Check It Out!**
Go to **http://bit.ly/Z74TpY** (case sensitive) where I'll explain how to work with the *Vortex Sort* template.

SMART Tip

Guess what? There are image versions of this template too. They are located in the same part of the *Gallery* as *Vortex Sort*, and they're called *Vortex Sort (image)*.

Think of the Possibilities

After you've used this activity with your class as a whole, make it available to your students during a center or anchor activity time. The self-checking feature makes it perfect for independent work. Any other vowel sort will work here too!

In math class, students might sort expressions that match a particular sum or difference, or you might ask your young scientists to sort living and nonliving things. Word lovers will enjoy sorting parts of speech or words that fit into one word family or another.

SMART Tools and
Techniques

SMART Tools and Techniques

Customizing the *Dice - Keyword* template

Roll and Write

The interactive dice in this activity make it more like a game than a skill review! One tap of the colorful die shows each example that students will interact with. The good news here is that these dice are programmable, so you can add any content you want from any subject you teach! Another piece of good news: This activity will also help your students build their knowledge of Numbers and Operations in Base Ten—Common Core style.

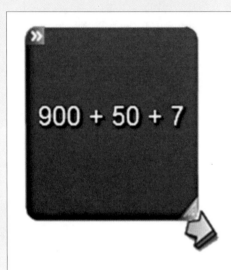

Materials

• Individual dry-erase boards
• Dry-erase markers

Before You Begin

Go to http://bit.ly/XaAmoK (case sensitive) and download the SMART Notebook file for this activity. Distribute the dry-erase boards and markers.

▶ **Check It Out!**
Go to **http://bit.ly/WqaA2y** (case sensitive) where I'll talk you through how to lead this activity.

Leading the Activity

◆ Open the SMART Notebook file to display the two blue dice. Ask students to bring their materials and gather in front of the board. Explain that their job will be to look at the expanded number displayed on the face of the die and figure out what number it represents.

◆ Tap the center of one die once to "roll" it. Once the face is displayed, ask students to write down the number they think is represented by the expanded form and then hold up their dry-erase boards so you can check their work.

◆ When most of your students are displaying their answers, choose a pen from the pen tray and write the correct number on the SMART Board. Ask students to check their answers. If anyone wrote an incorrect answer, take a moment to explain how to figure the correct response, using vocabulary and processes your math program suggests. When you're through, use the *Eraser* tool to clear away what you've written.

SMART Tip

If you want to make a die bigger or smaller, tap the resize button in the lower right corner of the die and drag in or out to the desired size.

- Continue with each of the dice until you have viewed all of the examples at least once.

- When you're through, close the file by tapping on the x in the upper right corner of the screen. Tap on *No* in the pop-up window.

Now You're the Wizard

In the *Gallery* tab, click on *Lesson Activity Toolkit*. Click on the blue bar titled *Interactive and Multimedia*. Scroll down to find the *Dice - Keyword* template (there's only one). Double-click or drag and drop the template onto your SMART Notebook page. To add words or numbers to the face of the die, click the double chevron in the upper left corner of the die. Type your content for each side in the bars. If you do not want the die to show the same content more than once, click on the small box in the lower right corner of the edit screen that says *No repeat*. Once your content is in place, click the double chevron again and you and your students are ready to roll! By the way, you can have as many dice on a page as you wish—just add more by the double-click or drag-and-drop method.

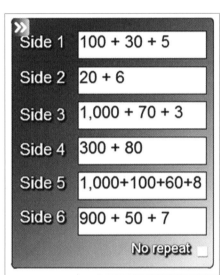

Side 1	100 + 30 + 5
Side 2	20 + 6
Side 3	1,000 + 70 + 3
Side 4	300 + 80
Side 5	1,000+100+60+8
Side 6	900 + 50 + 7

No repeat ☐

▶ Check It Out!

Go to **http://bit.ly/12TwtfH** (case sensitive) where I'll explain how to work with the *Dice - Keyword* template.

SMART Tip

This die interactive also has an image version. It's called *Dice - Image*. Instead of adding words in the spaces provided, you will drag and drop images from the *Gallery Essentials* into each space on the die. Don't worry about the size of the image—the software will make it fit perfectly!

Think of the Possibilities

This dice format is a fun way to practice rote skills such as sight words or number or letter recognition. Practice addition, subtraction, and multiplication facts by adding a single digit to each side and having two dice on the page. Tapping both dice will give you two numbers that students will then use to perform the operation you've dictated.

If your students' reading skills are up to it, type a word on each face of the die and ask students to determine its part of speech or the number of syllables it contains. To help your students break away from overusing certain words in their writing, put those "tired" words on a die and ask students to brainstorm synonyms.

SMART Tools and Techniques

Customizing the *Anagram* template

Bubble Wrap

A strong synonym vocabulary paves the way for terrific reading comprehension and fabulous written expression. The anagram format of this activity adds a bit of mystery, which your students will love. It's highly interactive both for students at the board and for students at their desks. This format works well with words in any content area.

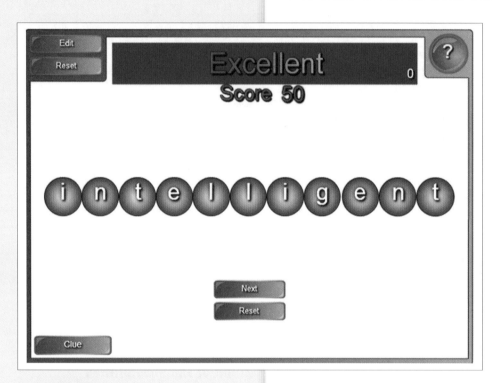

Before you Begin

Go to http://bit.ly/XLLQ5D (case sensitive) and download the SMART Notebook file for this activity.

▶ Check It Out!

Go to **http://bit.ly/13Ysnm2** (case sensitive) where I'll talk you through how to lead this activity.

Leading the Activity

◆ Open the SMART Notebook file to display the blank anagrams board. Ask students to gather in front of the board. Explain that their job will be to figure out what synonym for each clue word is displayed in scrambled form on the board. Then they'll need to direct you to put the letters of that word in the right order.

◆ Press the *Start* button. Demonstrate that when you press the *Clue* button, the clue word and anagram will appear on the screen and the timer will begin counting down. Explain that they don't need to worry about the timer. When they think they have figured out the scrambled word, they should stand up to indicate they're ready to make a guess.

◆ Once most of your students are standing, ask them to tell you what word they think it is. Then have them direct you to move the bubbles into the proper locations so that the word is spelled correctly. (Or ask for a volunteer to move the bubbles while his classmates direct him.)

◆ When the bubbles are in the correct order, the template will congratulate you and flash a score. Press the *Next* button and the *Clue* button to move onto the next anagram and repeat the process.

◆ When you're through, close the file by tapping on the x in the upper right corner of the screen. Tap on *No* in the pop-up window.

Now You're the Wizard

In the *Gallery* tab, click on *Lesson Activity Toolkit*. Click on the blue bar titled *Interactive and Multimedia*. Scroll down to find one of the *Anagram* templates. Double-click or drag and drop the template onto

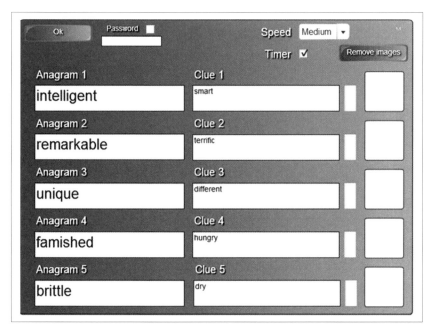

your SMART Notebook page. Click the *Edit* button on the template and type in your content. Note that you can turn the *Timer* feature on or off and choose the speed. Once you've filled the slots, click the *Ok* button and name and save the file.

▶ **Check It Out!**
Go to **http://bit.ly/ZL5ixb** (case sensitive) where I'll explain how to work with the *Anagram* template.

SMART Tip

The *Anagram* template has only five slots. If you want to create more anagrams, click on the *Add Page* icon and drag and drop an additional template onto the new page and fill it in as well.

Think of the Possibilities

Anagrams lend themselves to any kind of words: Use your weekly spelling words, math vocabulary, keywords from science textbooks or social studies units, or vocabulary words from a book you and your students are reading.

You can also set up the template with math equations instead of words so that students can practice math facts or greater-than or less-than skills. (Your students' task will be to put the numbers and symbols in the correct order.) It's a great way to practice rote material like math facts!

The Cycle of Life

Life cycles are fun to study, with plenty of variety as you and your students learn about different kinds of organisms. They also provide additional opportunities to practice sequencing skills. In this activity, students move words and pictures as they reinforce their understanding of a bean's life cycle. It makes a nice follow-up to informational text you may have read with your students and helps them to hone their ability to read and understand graphics—both key parts of Common Core State Standards. Use this format to investigate the life cycle of frogs, butterflies, or any other plant or animal—even humans!

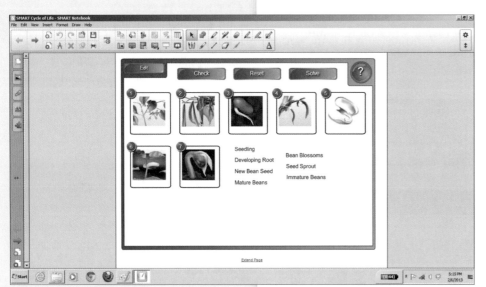

Materials

- Photocopies of the activity page, 1 for each student
- Glue
- Scissors
- Sentence strips

Before You Begin

Go to http://bit.ly/XzQzJT (case sensitive) and download the SMART Notebook file for this activity. Distribute the materials to your students.

▶ Check It Out!

Go to **http://bit.ly/XaD2me** (case sensitive) where I'll talk you through how to lead this activity.

Leading the Activity

◆ Open the SMART Notebook file to display the numbered images of the bean life cycle. Ask students to bring their materials and join you in front of the board. Explain that their job will be to place the pictures and labels in the correct order.

◆ One at a time, invite volunteers to come to the board and to drag the images to arrange them in correct order—with each volunteer changing the order of one image. Direct the rest of the class to cut out the pictures on their label sheet and paste them in order on the sentence strip.

◆ When the students' work at the board is finished, review with the class. If any of the images are out of order, discuss why and make needed corrections. Once your students have agreed that the order is correct, press the *Check* button at the top of the page. Repeat this checking step as needed until all steps are in the correct order.

◆ Next, read each word on the page to your students.

- Again, ask for volunteers to place each label with the correct image. Direct the rest of the class to cut out the labels and paste them in the proper spots on their sentence strips.

- The labels are not part of the template, so they cannot be checked with the *Check* or *Solve* button. You'll have to be the labels "checker." Be sure students check their individual work with the final product on the board.

- When you're through, close the file by tapping on the x in the upper right corner of the screen. Tap on *No* in the pop-up window.

Now You're the Wizard

In the *Gallery* tab, click on *Lesson Activity Toolkit*. Click on the blue bar titled *Interactive and Multimedia*. Scroll down to one of the *Image Arrange* templates. Double-click it or drag and drop it onto your page.

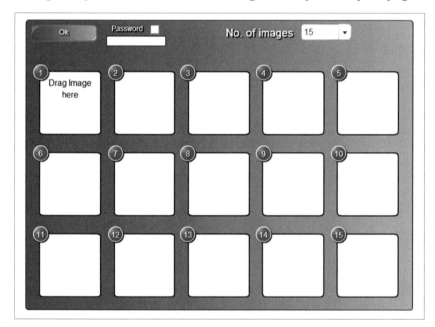

To add content to the template, click on the blue *Edit* button at the top left of the page. Decide how many images you want—15 is the maximum. You can search for images in the *Gallery*, copy and paste photos from your own files, or search for images on the Internet (be sure to avoid images that are copyright protected). Drag and drop images into the numbered boxes—the software will resize them automatically. Be sure to place the images in correct order. When you press the *Ok* button, the software will automatically rearrange them.

Next, click on the *Text* tool in your toolbar, and then click on the blank portion of the page to produce a text box. Type in one label. Repeat to add the rest of the labels. Name and save the file.

Think of the Possibilities

Life cycles are just one application of this template. You can also arrange events in a chapter or story you and your students have read or important events in a notable time in history. Inventions relating to something specific, like transportation, or a selection of those that are relevant to your students can also be discussed and placed in order. There are lots of choices here, so have fun!

▶ Check It Out!

Go to **http://bit.ly/ZCSjwj** (case sensitive) where I'll explain how to work with the *Image Arrange* template.

SMART Tip

The *Gallery* tab has its own search capabilities. To perform a search, open the tab, type your search term in the white search box at the top of the tab, and click on the magnifying glass to the right of the search box. Scroll down through the pictures to find images that are just right for you.

In the Driver's Seat— Build Pages from Scratch

Creating a SMART Notebook page from scratch is a fun and satisfying experience. I'm not joking, and I speak from experience—I've whipped up dozens of effective and unique SMART Board lessons. In this section of the book, I'll be right there to take you through every stage of the process with step-by-step instructions for creating 16 customizable activities. So while you explore the features and tools in the software and learn how they work, you also create. The fruition of your learning each time is an activity that you can use with your students.

To enhance your learning, you can access the online voice-over demonstrations, where you'll be able to watch each page being constructed as I explain the process. (Look for Check It Out! to find the Web addresses for the demonstrations.) I'll start with pages that are very simple to make using the most basic SMART Notebook tools and features. From there, the complexity builds a little as I show you how to work with additional features and the different layers of a SMART Notebook page to create some magical effects. Don't worry; it's nothing you can't handle! At any time, if you need extra information about a tool or technique mentioned in the instructions for creating an activity, refer to the Wizard's Guide on page 160, where you'll find concise explanations of SMART tools and techniques and how to use them.

The activities I'll take you through cover content from language arts and math to science and social studies. But the specific content I've chosen for these activity pages is just one example of how to use each one. All of them can be adapted for a variety of content and grade levels. I am confident that once you start realizing what SMART Notebook tools and features can do, you will begin imagining possibilities far beyond the scope of the specific activities in this book—which is, of course, the whole point! So enjoy the discovery of all the software has to offer and the fun of unleashing your creativity as you become a Totally SMART SMART Board user.

Keep working SMARTer as you learn how to design SMART Notebook activity pages that are just right for your students.

Correct the Teacher

Let's face it: Most students won't jump for joy when you tell them they need to do some proofreading. But that will change when it's *your* writing they are correcting and when they can execute their proofreading changes using the SMART Board. This activity is designed to give students a quick shot of practice with the conventions of the English language each day. The focus here is on proper punctuation, but you can design similar exercises to test students' mastery of almost any convention of written language. It will even help you assess your students' mastery of some of the Language and Writing standards of the Common Core State Standards. This would make a great start to your language block each day!

Last year my family went to a lake for vacation? It was the worst week of my life My sister teased me and! it rained all week..I think even my mom, and dad were bored I hope next year we can stay home. and camp out in the back yard.

Materials
- Photocopies of the activity page, 1 for each student
- Colored pens

Before You Begin
Create your own customized version of this activity page by following the instructions beginning on page 78. Distribute the photocopies and colored pens.

▶ **Check It Out!**
Go to **http://bit.ly/XaD3X7** (case sensitive) where I'll talk you through how to lead this activity.

Leading the Activity

◆ Open the SMART Notebook file you've created to display the text your students will be proofreading. Ask them to bring their materials and gather in front of the board. Explain that this is a paragraph that you wrote, and read the text aloud to them.

◆ Direct their attention to the Magic Number in the star in the upper right corner of the page. Explain that this number indicates how many punctuation errors there are in the paragraph. Tell them that, for example, you may have used incorrect punctuation marks or simply forgotten some.

◆ Challenge them to find your mistakes by scanning their papers and circling any items they think are incorrect. Allow them about five minutes to do this. (Keep in mind that they may not find all the errors.)

- Ask for a volunteer to come to the board and correct one of the mistakes using a *Pen* tool. In some cases, there may be more than one acceptable answer (a period or an exclamation point might work equally well at the end of a sentence, for example). If you see more than one possible answer, ask the student to justify why she made the choice she did. Then discuss the other possible answer and why it's also an acceptable choice.

- Once she's made the correction, ask your students to raise their hand if they agree; then select at least one student to explain why the correction was needed.

- If very few or no students raise their hand, ask why they *disagree*. This is a great opportunity for dialogue involving critical thinking and sharing opinions and knowledge.

- If the correction was unnecessary or incorrect, revise it as needed, explaining why you are doing so. Have students make the correction on their papers also if needed.

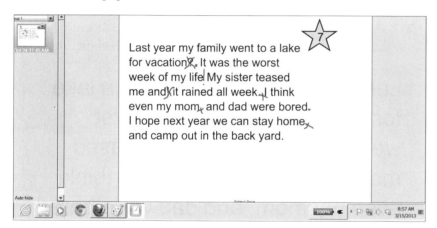

- Invite another student to come forward and correct another error. Repeat the process until all of the errors have been corrected. If your students have missed one of your errors entirely, point it out, explain why it's a mistake, and then ask their help in fixing it.

- When you're through, close the file by tapping on the x in the upper right corner of the screen. Tap on *No* in the pop-up window.

Think of the Possibilities

Correcting the teacher's mistakes is an activity that works well with almost any convention of written language, including correct spelling of words that belong to the same family or a review of multiple word families. You could write a fun paragraph that uses current spelling words, with some of the words deliberately misspelled. If your students aren't ready to read an entire paragraph, simply create exercises using single sentences instead.

SMART Tip

It's easy to adapt this exercise for students to use independently as a center. Set up the SMART Board with the original page displayed. Show your class where the *Clear Ink*

Clear Ink

tool is in the toolbar at the top of the page. Explain that once they've corrected all the errors and written their name on the page, they should print it out and then click on the *Clear Ink* tool. All of their marks will magically disappear, leaving the page ready for the next student.

Building the *Correct the Teacher* Page

◐ Check It Out!
Go to **http://bit.ly/16v3OMX** (case sensitive) where I'll talk you through
how to build this SMART Notebook page step by step.

1. Open a new SMART Notebook file by double-clicking on the
    SMART Notebook icon on your desktop. On scrap paper, jot down
    a paragraph or sentences you want your students to interact with.
    Remember to include some errors for them to correct!

2. Click on the *Text* tool. Choose a font and the size and color you
    like—this is similar to working with fonts in a word processing
    program. For this exercise, a dark color is best because it's easier
    to read. A larger font also works well because it provides more
    space for marking corrections. I used Arial 36.

3. Click anywhere on the page
    to produce a text box. Type in
    the text you composed in
    Step 1.

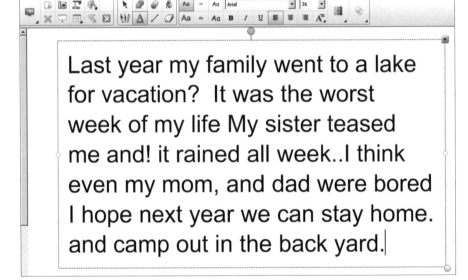

Last year my family went to a lake for vacation? It was the worst week of my life My sister teased me and! it rained all week..I think even my mom, and dad were bored I hope next year we can stay home. and camp out in the back yard.

4. Next, click on the *Shapes* tool; the shapes menu will appear. Click on the star.

Shapes

5. Bring your cursor onto the page and click and drag to make a star near the upper right corner of the page. The star should be large enough that you can type a number inside it.

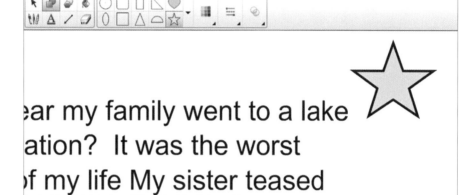

ear my family went to a lake ation? It was the worst f my life My sister teased

6. Click on the *Text* tool and then click on your star. A text box will appear inside the star. Type the number that corresponds to the number of errors in your text. (My example has seven errors, so I typed a 7 in the star.)

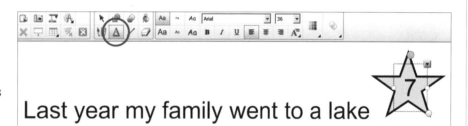

Last year my family went to a lake for vacation? It was the worst

7. Believe it or not, you're done! Name and save your file. If you think you might make a lot of these proofreading exercises, you might wish to include the convention you focused on in the file name. For example, you might call this one Correct the Teacher Punctuation.

SMART Tip

The default color of the star is gold, but you can change its color at any time. Click on the star on your page to select it—a blue frame should appear around the star.

Click on the *Properties* tab. Select the *Solid Fill* option, and then experiment by clicking on colors displayed in the color palette until you find one you like. Be sure to save the change!

SMART Tools and Techniques

Importing and resizing images

What's the Weather?

Matching up weather symbols with oral clues plus adjusting the temperature reading on an interactive thermometer will get your students talking like meteorologists. This activity is a great addition to your study of seasonal weather but can also serve as a fun segue into conversations about adjectives, idioms, and common sayings. Plus, it builds listening comprehension and critical thinking skills!

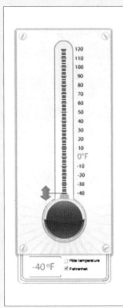

▶ Check It Out!
Go to **http://bit.ly/10MhfUE** (case sensitive) where I'll talk you through how to lead this activity.

Materials
- Photocopies of the activity page, 1 for each student
- Scissors

Before You Begin
Create your own customized version of this activity page following the instructions beginning on page 82. Prepare some notes for yourself with various weather clues to read during the activity. End each clue with the question, "What's the weather?" For example, one clue might be: "It's July and there's not a cloud in the sky. It's the hottest day of the year. What's the weather?" Distribute the photocopies and scissors, and ask students to cut out the weather symbols.

Leading the Activity

◆ Open the SMART Notebook file you've created to display the page of weather symbols and the interactive thermometer. Ask your students to bring their materials and come to the area in front of the board. Explain that their first job will be to listen to the clue. When you say "What's the weather?" they should hold up the weather symbol they think matches best. Their next job will be to help you figure out what the temperature might be and show that temperature on the thermometer.

◆ Show your students how to adjust the temperature on the interactive thermometer by pressing the double-headed arrow on the thermometer, dragging it up or down, and releasing it at the desired temperature.

- Read your first clue and watch to see that your students hold up a symbol when you say "What's the weather?" Lead a discussion of which symbols students are holding up and why. Ask a student to come to the board and drag the correct symbol or symbols to the center of the white space to the right of the thermometer.

- Now ask students to help you figure out what the temperature might be on a day like this one. Once determined, ask a volunteer to set that temperature on the thermometer.

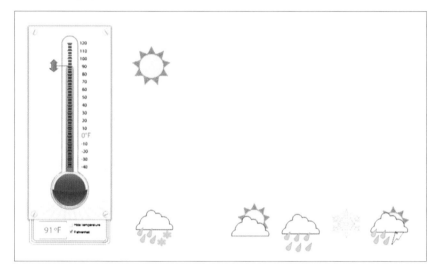

- Repeat the exercise with each of your clues. Point out that it's okay to repeat the use of a symbol.

- When you're through, close the file by tapping on the x in the upper right corner of the screen. Tap on *No* in the pop-up window.

SMART Tip

The temperature is displayed as a numeral at the base of the thermometer; the number changes as you move the arrow. If you want your students to figure that out by themselves, tap the *Hide Temperature* box at the base of the thermometer.

Think of the Possibilities

The quickest way to change up this activity is to change the symbols you use. The more closely the symbols resemble each other, the more critical thinking and careful listening your students will have to do. So go back to that *Gallery* tab and get searching!

Add a drop of fun to this activity by introducing weather idioms such as "It's raining cats and dogs." Ask students to match a symbol or picture to each idiom. You can search for weather images on the Internet too, but avoid downloading copyrighted images.

Building the *What's the Weather?* Page

▶ Check It Out!

Go to **http://bit.ly/WKcdug** (case sensitive) where I'll talk you through how to build this SMART Notebook page step by step.

1. Open a new SMART Notebook file by double-clicking on the SMART Notebook icon on your desktop.

2. Click on the *Gallery* tab; a search box will appear at the top of the tab. Type "weather" in the search box and click the magnifying glass. Search results will appear in the tab.

3. Click on the blue bar titled *Interactive and Multimedia*. The image labeled *Thermometer* is an interactive thermometer. Double-click the image to add it to your page.

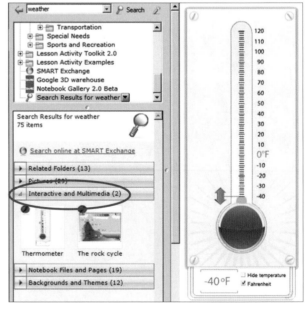

4. Another blue bar in the *Gallery* tab is called *Pictures*. Click on it, and then scroll down to look at the weather symbol options. Drag and drop any you want to use. Try to use a variety of weather types. I chose six for my page, all of similar artistic style.

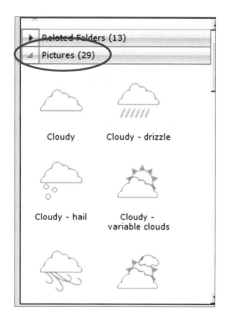

5. Resize each image after moving it if needed. (The resize button is in the lower right corner of each image when you first import it to the page.) Line up the symbols along the bottom of the page.

6. Your page is ready to use. Name and save the file.

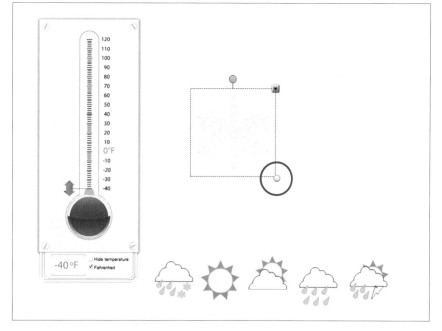

SMART Tip

You can click on the lower right-hand corner of the thermometer and drag your mouse out to make the thermometer larger. Make it as big as your page will allow. To make the thermometer display the temperature in degrees Fahrenheit (rather than Celsius), put a check mark in the box at the bottom of the thermometer.

SMART Tools and Techniques

Finding, importing, sizing, and cloning images

Working with the *Gallery* tab, *Add Page* tool, and *Pens* tool

Number-Story Station

Stimulate your students' ability to create and tell number stories and develop equations that match those stories with this picture-based activity. You can use this to help your students build the skills using all four mathematical operations and algebraic thinking, so it's very relevant to Common Core State Standards. SMART Notebook software offers an almost endless picture supply; if you wish, you can choose pictures related to the season or a theme of your choice.

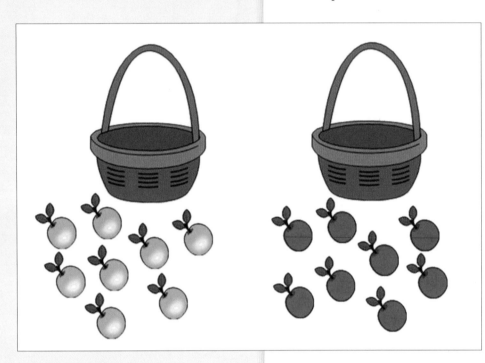

Materials

- Counters (such as plastic bingo chips or pennies)
- Individual dry-erase boards, 1 for each student
- Dry-erase markers

Before You Begin

Create your own customized version of this activity page following the instructions beginning on page 86. Distribute the counters, dry-erase boards, and markers.

▶ Check It Out!

Go to **http://bit.ly/ZQn1FM** (case sensitive) where I'll talk you through how to lead this activity.

SMART Tip

Add Page

With this activity, try using the *Add Page* tool when you're working with your students and you want to write out equations. That way, you can refer back to earlier work if you wish. When you close the file at the end of instruction, however, do not save the changes.

Leading the Activity

◆ Open the file to display the number-story images. Tell students that they will create a number story based on the pictures on the board. Remind them that a math story consists of at least two sentences and a question, and that there is more than one possible number story for each picture. Encourage creativity! If you wish, you can specify which operation students should use in their stories.

◆ Drag two of the green apples to one basket and one red apple to the other. Ask students to raise their hand and offer suggestions to help you create a story and equation that match what shows on the screen. For example: There were 2 green apples in one basket. There was 1 red apple in the other basket. How many apples were there in all? 2 + 1 = 3.

◆ Next, invite your students to create other number stories using the apples and baskets in any way they choose. Suggest that they use their counters and dry-erase boards to record their ideas. Then ask for a volunteer to come to the board and share her story by moving the objects on the board as necessary.

◆ Ask the rest of your students to write an equation that matches the number story and then hold up their boards for you to see.

◆ Together, review the story, orally creating an equation for it. Ask the storyteller to write that equation on the SMART Board using a *Pen* tool. (Erase the equation before you move on.)

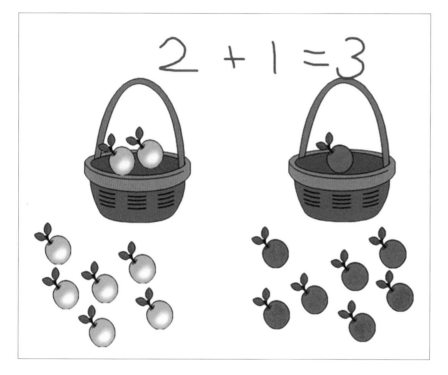

◆ Next, encourage students to come up with a new number story about the baskets and apples using a different operation. Or, if you've created more than one page, you can move on at this point.

◆ When you're through, close the file by tapping on the x in the upper right corner of the screen. Tap on *No* in the pop-up window.

Think of the Possibilities

You can use this activity for multiplication practice too. Just adapt the page by adding one or two more baskets; place the same number of apples in each basket. Give students graph paper on which they can make arrays to help them solve the problem. You might also encourage students to make fact families using the numbers in the original equation. Division, or "sharing," problems are an option as well.

Carry this activity over to language arts by having your students write out the number stories in words on the SMART Board—a sharing of the pen so to speak.

SMART Tip

Students can also create number stories on the SMART Board during a center or anchor activity time. Display a page from the Number-Story Station file on the board, and show students how to click on the page thumbnail in the *Page Sorter* tab and choose the *Clone* option (as described in Step 4 on page 86). Then they can move the objects and write a story or an equation to match right on the SMART Notebook page (make sure they write their name on the page too). Also show them how to save the file by clicking on the *Save* button in the toolbar. That way you'll be able to review their work at a later time.

Building the *Number-Story Station* Page

▶ Check It Out!
Go to **http://bit.ly/13Yx2o9** (case sensitive) where I'll talk you through how to build this SMART Notebook page step by step.

1. Open a new SMART Notebook file by double-clicking on the SMART Notebook icon on your desktop.

2. Click on the *Gallery* tab. Type "basket" in the search box, and click on the magnifying glass next to the search box. When the search results appear, click on the blue bar titled *Pictures*. Select the picture of the empty basket, and drag and drop it onto your Notebook page.

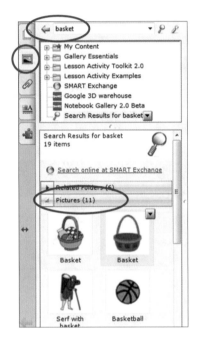

3. Size the basket as you wish by clicking on the resize button in the lower right corner of the frame around the basket. Hold and drag in or out; release your mouse when the basket is the size you desire.

4. Next, clone the basket by clicking on the gray menu arrow at the upper right corner of the frame and choosing the *Clone* option in the drop-down menu. Now you should have two identical baskets. Click and drag the new basket to space them as you wish.

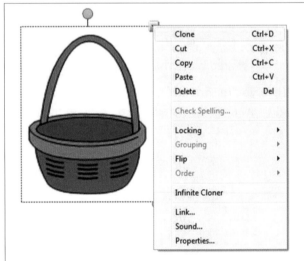

5. Go back to the *Gallery* and type "apple" in the search box. When the search results appear, open the blue *Pictures* bar and drag the image of the green apple onto your page.

6. Size the apple (as you did the basket in Step 3) so that several apples could fit in a basket. Then clone the apple as many times as you wish.

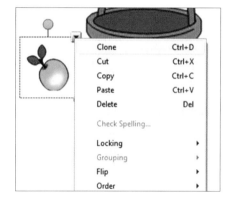

7. Drag the red apple image onto your page, and size and clone it in the same way.

8. If you want to add another page, click the *Add Page* button, which you'll find both in your toolbar and in the lower corner of your screen on whichever side your tabs are located. Search the *Gallery* for other images that might inspire your students, and repeat the process above.

Add Page

9. When you're done, name and save the file.

SMART Tip

If you don't have anything specific in mind to search for, just open the *Gallery* tab, choose the blue *Pictures* bar, and scroll through the items available. It's a great way to see what's there—and there's a lot!

SMART Tools and Techniques

Working with the *Table* tool and options

Mystery Number

Build number sense with this Mystery Number activity. This exercise will help students learn directionality in counting as well as those important mental math pieces that come from understanding numbers and their relationship to each other. The example below uses the numbers 121 to 170, but you can change the activity to focus on the range of numbers of your choice.

121	122	123	124	125	126	127	128	129	130
131	132	133	134	135	136	137	138	139	140
141	142	143	144	145	146	147	148	149	150
151	152	153	154	155	156	157	158	159	160
161	162	163	164	165	166	167	168	169	170

▶ Check It Out!

Go to **http://bit.ly/ZqZ6Lb** (case sensitive) where I'll talk you through how to lead this activity.

Materials

- Photocopies of the number chart, 1 for each student
- Counters (such as plastic bingo chips or pennies), 1 for each student

Before You Begin

Create your own customized version of this activity page following the instructions beginning on page 90. Distribute the photocopies and the counters to your class. If you're not familiar with the *Highlighter Pen* tool, turn to page 163 to learn more about it.

Leading the Activity

♦ Open the file to display the Mystery Number chart.

♦ Decide on the "mystery number." This is the number that your students should wind up at when the game reaches its conclusion. Write down the number on a piece of paper, and cover it with a second sheet of paper or other covering.

♦ Explain that you will be asking your students a series of questions that will require them to use various math skills to figure out the mystery number hidden behind the cover. They will use their charts to keep track of their answers as they go along.

♦ Pose a math problem you want your students to solve. Be sure to use math vocabulary words your students need to know. For example, you could say: "If I started at 123 and added 6, what number would I end up on?"

♦ Direct your students to place their counters on the number 123 on their charts and then figure the problem. When they have reached an answer, ask them to signal you by giving a thumbs-up. Once most of your students have the solution, ask a volunteer to come to the board and show or tell the group how he solved the problem, using the *Highlighter Pen* tool to show the moves on the chart.

121	122	123	124	125	126	127	128	129	130
131	132	133	134	135	136	137	138	139	140
141	142	143	144	145	146	147	148	149	150
151	152	153	154	155	156	157	158	159	160
161	162	163	164	165	166	167	168	169	170

- Pose another question that builds on the answer to the first one, such as: "We're at 129. Where would I be if I added 14?"

- Repeat the process above, posing a new question each time, with students solving, signaling, and explaining how they arrived at the solution. Each new student who comes to the board should choose a different color of *Highlighter Pen* than the child before.

- Be sure you don't forget the mystery number, and make sure that the final question you ask will lead your students to the right number! Then you can remove the cover with a flourish to reveal the mystery number to your students.

- When you're through, close the file by tapping on the x in the upper right corner of the screen. Tap on *No* in the pop-up window.

Think of the Possibilities

As your students become more proficient at this activity, consider just giving them the tasks, and don't stop to discuss solutions and explanations. Once you've given all the clues, reveal the mystery number, and ask your students whether they actually arrived there.

Take a break from the Mystery Number game and use this chart to help your students practice compass directions. Ask them to put their counters on a specific number on the chart. Then give them directions for moving their counters using compass rose terms such as *north, west,* and *southeast.* For example, ask: "If you start on 128 and move south 3 spaces, where will you end up?" (The correct answer is 158.)

SMART Tip

To add extra challenge, try posing problems that require multiple operations (increase 7, subtract 3) or multiple steps (subtract 2, then go 5 fewer) in order to come up with the answer.

Building the *Mystery Number* Page

▶ Check It Out!

Go to **http://bit.ly/XLTdtQ** (case sensitive) where I'll talk you through how to build this SMART Notebook page step by step.

1. Open a new SMART Notebook file by double-clicking on the SMART Notebook icon on your desktop.

2. Click on the *Table* tool in your toolbar. Select the size table you'd like to make by dragging your mouse across the array of boxes. Since this activity involves numbers, it's best to make it 10 columns wide. For this example, I used five rows, but once you see how this works, you can make a table of whatever dimensions you wish.

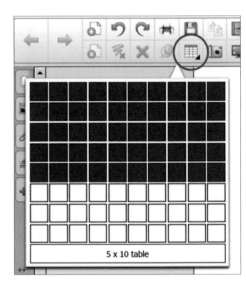

5 x 10 table

3. Once your table has the correct number of columns and rows, release your mouse. The table will appear on your screen with a blue frame around it. To move the table around on the page, position your cursor just inside the blue frame until it turns into a four-headed arrow, then click and drag it. (To move it again in the future, first click outside the table and drag your cursor across the table until the blue frame appears around it.)

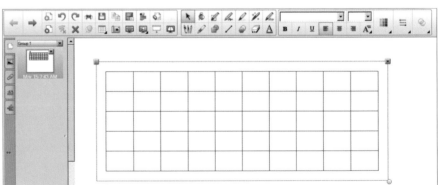

4. To add a number inside any given cell of the table, just click on that cell. It will turn color and a drop-down menu arrow will appear in the upper right corner. Text options will open up in your toolbar too. Essentially what you've done is open a text box inside that cell of the table. You can choose the font and the size and color you want the text in that cell to be. You can also center-justify the text if you wish.

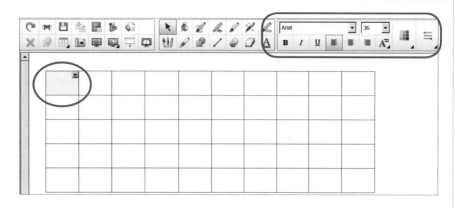

5. To set the same type options for the entire table, select the whole table by clicking and dragging across it. Then choose the text options you wish. Click outside the table to deselect it. Type your starting number in the first box. Repeat with all of the other boxes in the table. In this example, I started the table at the number 121. If you need to fix a typing error inside any cell, just double-click inside that cell and edit as usual.

121	122	123	124	125	126	127	128	129	130
131	132	133	134	135	136	137	138	139	140
141	142	143	144	145	146	147	148	149	150
151	152	153	154	155	156	157	158	159	160
161	162	163	164	165	166	167	168	169	170

6. Once the number chart is filled in, name and save the file.

SMART Tip

You can manipulate a table in SMART Notebook the same way you would a table in your word processing program. To adjust the width of any of the rows or columns, bring your cursor to any line, and it will turn into a double-headed arrow. Click and drag until the cells are the dimensions you want them to be.

SMART Tools and Techniques

Importing and resizing images

Working with the *Lines* and *Text* tools to create a simple chart

Complex Shape Sort

One of the best ways to make learning meaningful to students is to make connections to things they see and use every day. This activity will help your students find real-world connections to their geometry studies and the Geometry section of the Common Core State Standards. Plus, once you've worked through the activity at the SMART Board, you can repeat it using objects such as globes, puzzle boxes, or playground balls. Creating customized sorting charts like this one is a breeze; use your imagination to devise sorting exercises for every subject area.

cylinder	cube	sphere	rectangular prism	

Before You Begin

Create your own customized version of this activity page following the instructions beginning on page 94.

► **Check It Out!**
Go to **http://bit.ly/13VqRRa** (case sensitive) where I'll talk you through how to lead this activity.

Leading the Activity

♦ Open the SMART Notebook file to display the sorting chart. Ask students to gather in front of the board. Explain that their task is to match each object on the board with the correct shape name.

♦ Read the headings for each column in the table, and review the names of the objects pictured.

♦ Ask for a volunteer to come to the board, touch an image, and drag it to the correct column in the table. (For example, the image of the bottle would be placed into the cylinder column.)

♦ Verify that the shape is in the correct column.

♦ Direct the rest of the class to look around the classroom and spot something that has the same shape. Give them time to look, then give a signal, explaining that now they can go and stand beside the object they've spotted. (Depending on what shapes you've chosen for the chart, you might have to plant a few items around your room. Most classrooms don't have many pyramids on hand, for example!)

◆ Check in with a few students, and draw the group's attention to the objects spotted and confirm that they exhibit the correct shape. Then ask everyone to return to the area in front of the board.

cylinder	cube	sphere	rectangular prism	

◆ Repeat the process until you've sorted all the items on the board (but notice that a few of the shapes do not fit any of the categories).

◆ When you're through, close the file by tapping on the x in the upper right corner of the screen. Tap on *No* in the pop-up window.

Think of the Possibilities

You can vary this activity by saving a version of this page with all of the objects sorted into columns—but not necessarily in the correct spot. It will be your students' job to discern which images are in the correct place and which are not.

Ask questions to direct the discussion, such as "Why do you think this image should stay here?" or "Why do you want to move this object to a different spot?" This is a good exercise in critical thinking and review of the concept. For example, a student might say that an image doesn't belong with the cylinders because it doesn't have any round faces.

Building the *Complex Shape Sort* Page

▶ Check It Out!
Go to **http://bit.ly/Z75Tug** (case sensitive) where I'll talk you
through how to build this SMART Notebook page step by step.

1. Open a new SMART Notebook file by double-
    clicking on the SMART Notebook icon on
    your desktop. Decide how many columns your
    shape-sorting chart will have and what your
    column headings will be.

2. Click on the *Lines* tool and bring your cursor onto
    the page. It will appear as crosshairs. Begin making
    the vertical divider lines for the chart. Position your
    cursor at the spot where a line should start. Click
    and drag until you've reached the spot where you
    want your line to stop. Repeat
    this action to make all the
    columns. Leave some open
    space to one side of the chart
    (for images).

Lines

3. Next, add one horizontal line
    across the top to complete the
    chart structure.

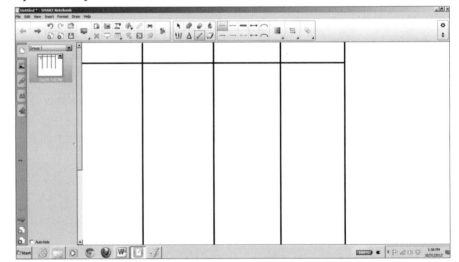

4. Now you'll need to add a text heading for each col-
    umn. Click on the *Text* tool, then click in one of the
    heading spaces. Type in the column headings.

Text

5. If you want to reposition a heading, click on the *Select* tool and then on the text box and drag it to where you want it to be. To make the word smaller, click on the small gray button in the lower right corner of the text box and drag in toward the text.

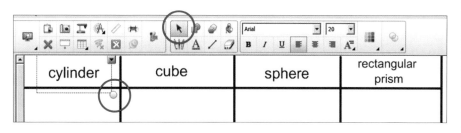

cylinder	cube	sphere	rectangular prism

6. Now you'll need some pictures for your students to sort. This will take a little hunting depending on what shapes you are looking for and how many of each you want. Click on the *Gallery* tab and type "shapes" in the search box. Click on the magnifying glass, and search results will appear in the tab.

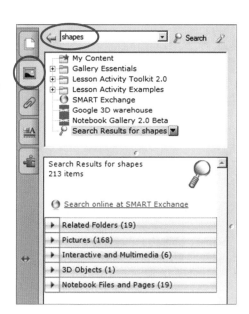

SMART Tip

In the *Gallery* tab under *Gallery Essentials,* you'll see the word *Mathematics*. Click on it. In the drop-down menu that appears, click on *Shapes, Space,* and *Measure*. This will bring up some additional images that your first search did not.

Building the *Complex Shape Sort* Page *continued*

7. Click on the blue bar titled *Pictures.* Scroll down through the images. When you find one you like, double-click it to import it onto your SMART page.

8. If needed, resize it using the resize button at the lower right corner of the blue frame. Click and drag in to make the image smaller or out to make it bigger.

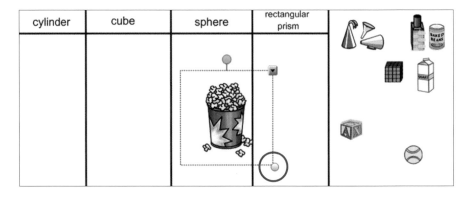

9. Continue until you have found all the images you want. You can also narrow your search by searching specific keywords that have the shape you want, such as "soup can" or "ice cream cone." Feel free to be a little flexible in your choices of images. For example, a snowman can work if you ask your students to focus on what its parts are made of (spheres).

10. Your page is ready to go! Be sure to name and save the file.

Fabulous Field Trip

Go out into the big wide world without ever leaving your classroom! In this exercise, you'll take your students on a virtual tour of the Statue of Liberty. Once you know the process of setting up a virtual tour, you can set up tours related to nearly any subject area. You'll also discover how easy it is to launch Internet resources of all kinds by simply tapping your SMART Board.

Before You Begin

Create your own customized version of this activity page following the instructions beginning on page 99. Be sure you are connected to the Internet. Take time to visit the tour website first on your own and learn its ins and outs, its extras, and its navigational quirks.

SMART Tools and Techniques

Importing and resizing images and using the *Link* technique

Leading the Activity

◆ Open the file you created to display the picture of the Statue of Liberty. Tap the globe icon in the lower left corner of the picture. The Web page will open and a short musical introduction will play before you reach page 1 of the tour, or you can click on the arrows to skip the introduction.

◆ Ask for a volunteer to come to the board and press some of the buttons and options for the first page of the tour. On each page of the tour, there may be additional video, some commentary from a park ranger, close-up images of the statue, links to more information, and so on. Stop for conversations, observations, and the opportunity to ask and answer questions. In other words, act as though you are on a field trip—because you are!

▶ **Check It Out!**
Go to **http://bit.ly/151Z91o** (case sensitive) where I'll talk you through how to lead this activity.

Think of the Possibilities

When using a virtual tour, I like to embed it in a file that contains other pages of related activities. For example, this page might be part of a multipage SMART Notebook file that includes an activity page from the *Lesson Activity Toolkit* highlighting relevant vocabulary, a page with an image of the Statue of Liberty that students can label using a *Pen* tool, and a page with a graph of statistics from Ellis Island.

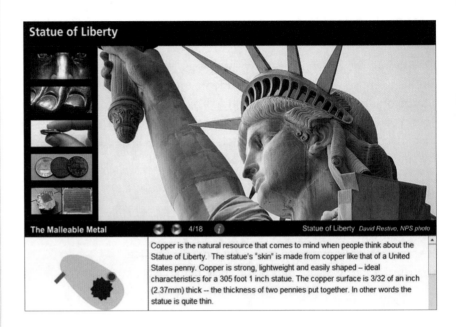

- ◆ Invite a second student to come to the board to explore page 2 of the tour. Strive to allow as many students as possible to interact with the board as the tour proceeds.

- ◆ When you're ready to end the tour, close the Internet browser by tapping the x in the upper right corner of the screen. This will bring you back to your SMART Notebook page. Close the file by tapping on the x in the upper right corner of the screen.

Building the *Fabulous Field Trip* Page

▶ Check It Out!

Go to **http://bit.ly/XA6UOL** (case sensitive) where I'll talk you through how to build this SMART Notebook page step by step.

1. Open a new SMART Notebook file by clicking on the SMART Notebook icon on your desktop.

2. Open the *Gallery* tab and type "lady liberty" in the search box. Then click on the magnifying glass next to the search box.

3. When the search results appear, click on the blue bar titled *Pictures.* You'll see a picture titled Lady Liberty.

4. To import the picture onto your page, double-click on the picture and it will automatically appear on your page. Or you can drag the thumbnail picture onto your page and drop it there.

SMART Tip

The quality of virtual tours varies greatly. Most virtual tours are free, but some organizations do charge a fee. The National Park Service is a good place to start. Its tours are high quality and free of charge. You can locate other virtual tours by using a search engine and the keywords "virtual field trips."

Building the *Fabulous Field Trip* Page *continued*

5. Once your picture is on the page, you may want to center it or change its size. To center it, click and drag the image where you want it and drop it. To resize the picture, use the resize button in the lower right corner. Drag it out to make the picture bigger, or drag it in to make the picture smaller.

6. Now it's time to link this image to the website you want to tour. This is the really cool part! Before you can link the picture to the site, you need the exact address of the Web page where the tour begins. To find that, use your Internet browser to navigate to the tour start page. Go to the address bar at the top of the page and highlight the Web address. Then right-click on your mouse and choose *Copy* in the drop-down menu. For the Statue of Liberty tour, I used the Web address www.nps.gov/featurecontent/stli/eTour.htm.

7. Back on your SMART page, click on the gray menu arrow at the upper right corner of the statue image. Choose the *Link* option from the drop-down menu.

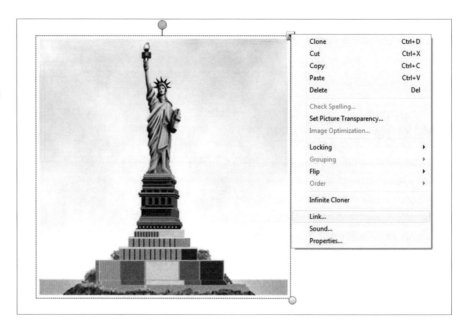

8. An *Insert Link* dialog box will appear. There are several options for linking; the first option is linking to a Web page. Make sure that option is selected by clicking on the Web Page icon.

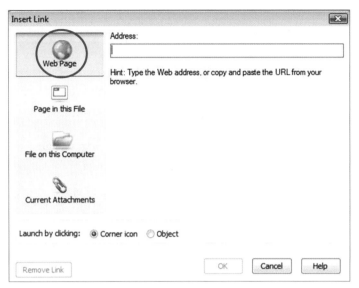

9. Click in the white address bar near the top of the box, then right-click and select *Paste*. The saved address from the Web page you just visited should appear in the white bar. Once it does, go ahead and click on the *OK* button at the bottom of the dialog box.

10. Now your picture of Lady Liberty is linked to the Web page that hosts the virtual tour. It's the magic of technology! Name and save your file. Anytime you open this page and tap on the little globe icon in the lower left corner of the picture, you will automatically be launched to this Web page (as long as you are connected to the Internet, of course).

SMART Tools and Techniques

Cloning pages to create a multipage "mystery word" activity

Working with the *Text* and *Screen Shade* tools and the *Page Sorter* tab

Super Spelling Shades

Students will love the element of mystery in this activity. It's a great interactive way to review the week's spelling words. Use it in a whole-group setting as described below, or allow your students to try it out on their own or with a classmate during an independent work time.

r e p

Materials
• Small dry-erase boards
• Dry-erase markers

Before You Begin
Create your own customized version of this activity page following the instructions beginning on page 104. Distribute the materials to the students.

▶ **Check It Out!**
Go to **http://bit.ly/13Yt3rw** (case sensitive) where I'll talk you through how to lead this activity.

Leading the Activity

◆ Open the SMART Notebook file you created to display the page with the screen shade in place. If you wish, ask students to bring their materials and gather in front of the board. Explain that one of the spelling words of the week is hidden behind the "shade" on the screen. Point out the dimple on the left side of the screen, and explain that touching and dragging the dimple will cause the screen to move, revealing the letters of the mystery word.

◆ Invite a volunteer to come to the board and drag the dimple to the right just enough to reveal one letter of the word in hiding.

◆ Direct your students to guess what the mystery word is and write it on their individual dry-erase boards.

◆ Ask the student at the SMART Board to reveal the next letter. Invite the rest of the class to erase their boards and make a new guess if needed, based on the letter that was just revealed.

◆ After two or three letters are visible (depending on the length of the words you are using), and students have finished writing their final guess, ask students to stand up with their boards facing you.

r e p l a c e

- Ask for a volunteer to call out the word he thinks is hidden behind the screen. Then ask the student at the board to reveal the word in its entirety.

- Direct the rest of the class to check the spelling of their guess against the word on the SMART Board and correct any mistakes they made.

- Move on to the next mystery word by tapping on its thumbnail view in the *Page Sorter* tab or by tapping the blue *Next Page* arrow in the toolbar. Invite a new student to come to the board, and repeat the exercise.

- Continue until you've viewed all the words in the file.

- When you're through, close the file by tapping on the x in the upper right corner of the screen. Tap on *No* in the pop-up window.

Think of the Possibilities

The mystery-word approach works equally well for reviewing vocabulary words from your reading series stories, science or social studies terms, or math vocabulary.

Educators who teach special populations could adapt this exercise so that the screen shade reveals half of a shape, a single letter, or a single number for students to identify rather than a spelling or vocabulary word.

Try using the screen shade with math facts too: Reveal the answer and one numeral in the problem plus the operation. Ask students to figure out the missing number in the equation.

Building the *Super Spelling Shades* Page

▶ Check It Out!

Go to **http://bit.ly/WKcAoz** (case sensitive) where I'll talk you through how to build this SMART Notebook page step by step.

1. Open a new SMART Notebook file by double-clicking on the SMART Notebook icon on your desktop. Decide on the list of words you want to use (spelling words, social studies terms, and so on).

2. Click on the *Text* tool and select the largest font size available—it's likely 72. Also choose the font and text color you'd like. An open font like Arial Black, Century Gothic, or Cornerstone will probably work best for this activity. Now click anywhere on the blank page and a text box will appear with a flashing cursor (vertical line) in it.

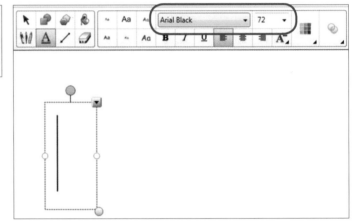

3. Type the first word, leaving an extra space (or two) between each letter. If you then want to reposition the text box, simply move your mouse around inside the box until it turns into a four-headed arrow. Then click and drag it where you want it to be.

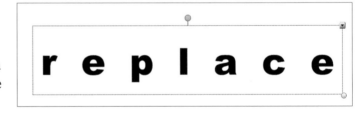

4. Click on the *Page Sorter* tab (or it may already be open on your screen). You should see a thumbnail of your newly created page in the tab area. Click on the drop-down menu button in the upper right corner of the thumbnail. Choose the *Clone Page* option in the menu.

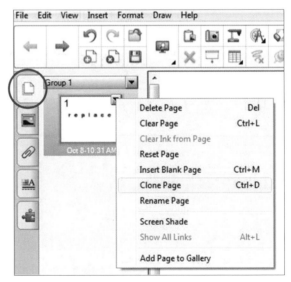

5. An identical thumbnail should appear directly below the first one in the *Page Sorter* tab. Click on that page to view it on your screen. The next task is to change the word to another word from your list. To do that, simply double-click on the text; a blue frame will appear around it. Be sure the word is highlighted, and start typing. Remember to leave an extra space or two between each letter.

6. Repeat this process to create a separate page for each word on your list.

7. Now to add the mystery. Click on the *Screen Shade* tool in your toolbar. When you do this, a dark gray shade will cover the entire page. Don't worry; that's what is supposed to happen! Do this for each page.

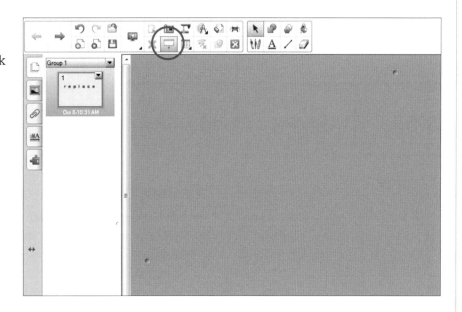

8. You're finished! Name and save the file. I recommend calling it something like Spelling Shades Unit 1. Then, if you make other Spelling Shade files for other lists, you can differentiate between them easily.

Smart Tip

You can also apply screen shades using the drop-down menus of the thumbnails in the *Page Sorter* tab. Simply open the drop-down menu for each thumbnail in turn and choose the *Screen Shade* option.

SMART Tools and Techniques

Importing and resizing images and applying the *Locking* and *Infinite Cloner* techniques

Working with the *Lines* and *Text* tools

Money Tic-Tac-Toe

Practice counting and creating coin combinations while playing a favorite game! This activity is flexible enough to use with students who are just learning to count coins as well as those with a higher level of skill. You can use this format not only with other math content, but also with many language arts skills, and it would perform well as a workstation!

$1.15	$0.75	$0.69
$0.41	$1.28	$0.37
$1.67	$0.96	$2.58

Before You Begin

Create your own customized version of this activity page following the instructions beginning on page 108.

▶ Check It Out!
Go to **http://bit.ly/16uZ5eh** (case sensitive) where I'll talk you through how to lead this activity.

Leading the Activity

◆ Open the file you created to display the Money Tic-Tac-Toe board. Divide your students into two teams, and ask the two groups to gather in front of the board. Explain to your students that they will be playing tic-tac-toe with a coin-counting twist. In order to claim a square on the playing board for the team, a player will first have to select coins that tally up to the total shown in the square she wishes to claim. Not only that, but she must use the *fewest* coins possible to reach the total. For example, if the amount shown in a square is $1.00, the player would have to select four quarters. Ten dimes would not meet the rules of play, even though ten dimes do equal $1.00.

◆ Direct the first player from Team X to choose one square on the board and then drag coins into that square to equal the total amount shown.

◆ Count his attempt aloud with your students. If it's correct, direct the student to use a *Pen* tool to make an X in the square he just filled with coins.

- If his attempt is not correct, take a moment to correct it, but then drag the coins back to their respective places.

- Invite a player from Team O to take a turn, following the same procedure.

$1.15	$0.75	
$0.41	$1.28	$0.37
$1.67		$2.58

- Continue play until one team achieves three in a row.

- Repeat the game until all players on both teams have had at least one turn if possible.

- When you're through, close the file by tapping on the x in the upper right corner of the screen. Tap on *No* in the pop-up window.

Think of the Possibilities

The list of possible placeholders for the squares in a tic-tac-toe board is almost endless. Here are just two ideas to start your brain juicing: Place math expressions in the squares; students must offer the correct answer before marking the square with an X or O. On the language arts side, try putting abbreviations, such as Mon., Dec., or Blvd., in each square. Students must correctly state what the abbreviation stands for in order to claim the square.

Building the *Money Tic-Tac-Toe* Page

▶ Check It Out!

Go to **http://bit.ly/WgkEMB** (case sensitive) where I'll talk you through how to build this SMART Notebook page step by step.

1. Open a new SMART Notebook file by double-clicking on the SMART Notebook icon on your desktop. Jot down the money amounts you will insert in the tic-tac-toe board, choosing amounts that are appropriate for your students' level.

2. Click on the *Lines* tool in your toolbar and then bring your cursor onto the page. It will appear as crosshairs. Make a traditional tic-tac-toe board on the page by bringing your cursor to the spot where you want to begin your line, and click and drag until your line is as long as you want (but leave some space open on the right side of the page for the coins). Release your mouse. Repeat to make each line of the tic-tac-toe board.

Lines

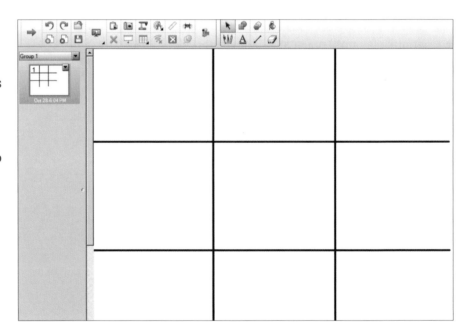

3. Now click on your *Text* tool, and then click in one box of the game board and type a money amount. Repeat this process in each of the other eight boxes, writing a different amount each time.

4. It's important to "lock" your board at this point; this keeps it stationary during use even when you and your students are dragging coins around the page. To do this, position your cursor just outside the upper left corner of the board. Click and drag across it until all the objects on the screen are highlighted by blue frames. Then click on the gray menu arrow at the top right corner of one frame, and choose *Locking* in the drop-down menu and then *Lock In Place*.

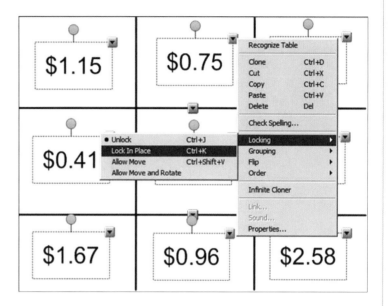

5. The next step is to add coins onto the page. Open the *Gallery* tab and type "quarter" into the search box. Click on the magnifying glass next to the search box. Click on the blue bar that reads *Pictures* and find the image of the front of a quarter. Import it onto your page by dragging and dropping it there or double-clicking on the image.

Building the *Money Tic-Tac-Toe* Page *continued*

6. Drag the image of the quarter to the right side of the page. Repeat the process to import a dime, nickel, and penny and position them along the right side of the page.

$1.15	$0.75	$0.69
$0.41	$1.28	$0.37
$1.67	$0.96	$2.58

7. Resize each coin to be a bit smaller by clicking on the coin and then the resize button in the lower right corner of the blue frame. Drag your cursor in slightly.

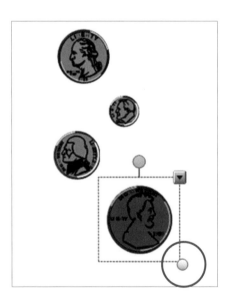

8. Now you use the *Infinite Cloner* feature so that your students will have access to unlimited numbers of each coin. First, select all the coins by clicking and dragging your cursor across the coins until a blue frame appears around each one.

9. Click on the gray menu arrow in the upper right corner of one of the blue frames. Choose *Infinite Cloner* from the options in the drop-down menu. You won't see any dramatic result, but now each of these coins can be repeatedly cloned and the clones will be movable.

10. Your page is ready! Be sure to name and save the file.

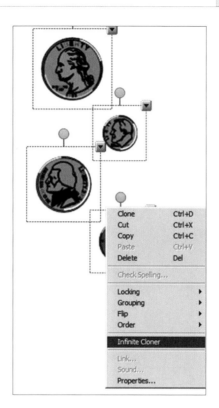

SMART Tip

If you create multiple pages like this one in the same file, you can simply switch pages when you and your students are ready to play the next game. To make this even easier, open the *Page Sorter* tab, right-click on the page in the tab, and choose *Clone Page* from the options. Then all you have to do is change the money amounts in each box and your new page is ready to use.

SMART Tools and Techniques

Searching, importing, and resizing images from the *Gallery* and the Internet

Working with the *Text* tool and the *Screen Capture* tool

Word-Choice Wonders

Strong vocabularies help students in so many areas—reading comprehension, writing acumen, and oral communication, just to name a few. With your SMART Board activity, you can use images of classic works of art to build your students' vocabularies. This type of page is simple to make, and you can use it for a variety of content areas just by changing the image. Your students will develop great vocabularies without even knowing it.

shiny

lacy

curious

ruffled

wavy

domed

captivated

Before You Begin

Create your own customized version of this activity page following the instructions beginning on page 114.

▶ Check It Out!

Go to **http://bit.ly/XaDzEl** (case sensitive) where I'll talk you through how to lead this activity.

Leading the Activity

◆ Open the SMART Notebook file to display the image and list of descriptive terms. Ask your students to gather in front of the SMART Board.

◆ Read the words you've listed on the right side of the page to your students. Explain that it will be their job to find one or more examples of each word in the picture. They will be using the *Screen Capture* tool to do so.

◆ Show your students where the *Screen Capture* tool is located on the toolbar, explain how to use it, and model use of the tool once for your students. (If you don't know how to use the *Screen Capture* tool, refer to the instructions below, Steps 8 through 10.)

◆ Read a word from the list (and define it if necessary), and ask for a volunteer to come to the board and capture something in the image that exemplifies the term.

- Once the student has captured a portion of the image, ask the group whether they agree with the student's choice. Encourage student discussion about why a word and a section of an image do or don't go together. The conversations you'll have with your students and those they'll have with each other during this exercise are just as valuable as the exercise itself!

- Thank the student, and then tap the thumbnail image of the page in the *Page Sorter* tab. Ask students if there are any other sections of the picture that might fit the word in question. If there are, ask a student to come up and do a screen capture. Once your students have located all other portions of the picture that match the word, drag the word from the right side of the page to the section of the picture it describes.

- Repeat the steps above for each word on the page.

- When you're through, close the file by tapping on the x in the upper right corner of the screen. Tap on *No* in the pop-up window.

Think of the Possibilities

Use this activity for science instruction by choosing an image of a pond, for example, or for a social studies discussion by selecting an image of George Washington crossing the Delaware.

There's no need to limit this to vocabulary practice either. For example, you can ask students to find portions of the image they can name by using a word that starts with the "m" sound or that contains three syllables. Or ask them to capture an important setting detail and explain what that detail is.

SMART Tip

To move your toolbar from the top to the bottom of the screen (or vice versa), click on the double-headed arrow on the far right side of the toolbar. This will help short students utilize the toolbar independently, and it will help you to do so more comfortably.

Building the *Word-Choice Wonders* Page

⏵ Check It Out!

Go to **http://bit.ly/16v4npZ** (case sensitive) where I'll talk you through how to build this SMART Notebook page step by step.

1. Open a new SMART Notebook file by double-clicking on the SMART Notebook icon on your desktop.

2. Open the *Gallery* tab and do some browsing. You're looking for an image that provides rich opportunities for description—something with lots of textures and interesting details. If you want to use the image I used here, type "don manuel" in the search box. Then click on the magnifying glass next to the search box.

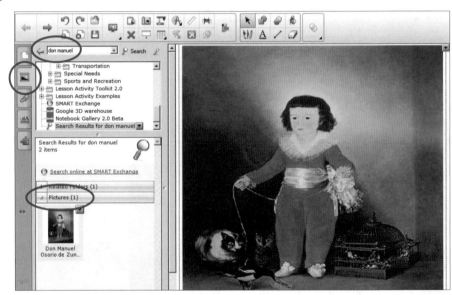

3. If you typed in "don manuel," you should see his portrait at the top of the tab. Drag and drop him onto your page. To make the image a bit bigger, click and drag the gray resize button in the lower right corner of the blue frame.

SMART Tip

While this example uses a picture from the *Gallery*, you can always import images of works of art from an Internet image search—just be sure to avoid copyrighted images. Once you've found an available image you like, right-click on it and choose the *Copy Image* option. Then return to your SMART page, right-click again, and choose the *Paste* option. The image will appear on your page.

4. Click on the *Text* tool. Choose the font and size you want your text to be. Or if you like the default, go for it. I used Arial 20.

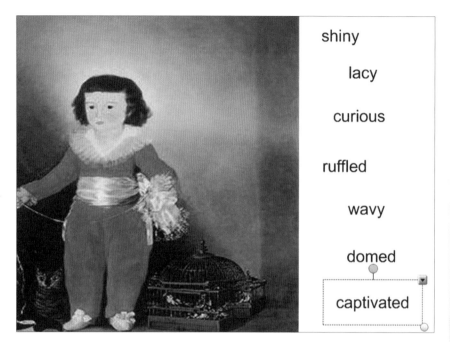

5. Think of a word or short phrase that describes something in the picture. Click on the white space to the right of the picture, and a text box will appear. Type in the word or phrase.

6. Click on the white space again to make another text box, and type the next word or phrase you think of. Repeat this for as many words as you'd like. The goal here isn't quantity of words, but quality: Strive for words that are a little sophisticated. The beauty of this activity is that your students don't need to be able to read or write the words, so you can make rich choices.

7. Now your page is ready for use, but you need to know one more very important thing—how to work with the *Screen Capture* tool your students will use when you do the activity together. So to keep this page safe from mishap while you practice with *Screen Capture*, name and save it now.

8. Open a new SMART Notebook file and import the same picture you just used or any other image from the *Gallery* or the Internet onto the page. If you use an image from the Internet, be sure to avoid copyrighted images.

Building the *Word-Choice Wonders* Page *continued*

9. Click the *Screen Capture* tool in your toolbar. The *Screen Capture* pop-up toolbar will appear on your screen. Click on the leftmost button, which I call *Click and Drag Capture*.

10. Your cursor will appear as crosshairs. Click and drag across the boy's face until it is surrounded by a black rectangle. Then release and wait for the magic. The section of the picture you captured will be copied and placed on another page within your Notebook file. Pretty cool, huh?

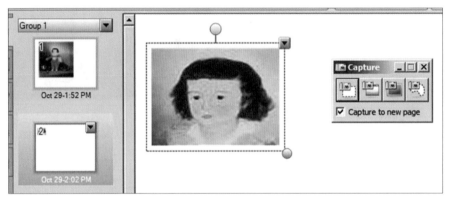

11. Capture the sections of the image that correlate to the words you chose—just for practice. Each time you capture another detail, it's inserted onto a new page in the file. You'll also notice that the *Screen Capture* toolbar stays active until you close it by clicking on the x in the upper right corner.

12. When you're finished practicing, close your practice file by clicking on the x in the upper right corner of the screen. Click on *No* in the pop-up window because this file was just for practice.

SMART Tip

You can activate the *Screen Capture* tool and then minimize the SMART Notebook page. When you do so, you'll see the *Screen Capture* toolbar is still on your screen. This allows you to capture sections of pictures on the Internet, portions of your desktop, really almost anything from anywhere, and it will be inserted into the SMART Notebook file you're working on.

Fraction Makers

Take the fear out of fractions with this hands-on opportunity to display fractional values and equivalencies using concrete materials. The ability to rotate the shapes and see through them stimulates critical thinking too, because students will need to think of more than one way to accomplish the task at hand. This activity is a great correlation to the Numbers and Operations—Fractions section of the Common Core State Standards.

SMART Tools and Techniques

Importing images and using the *Infinite Cloner* technique

Working with the *Shapes, Color,* and *Transparency* tools

Materials

- Photocopies of the activity page, several per student
- Scissors

Before You Begin

Create your own customized version of this activity page following the instructions beginning on page 119. Distribute the photocopies and scissors, and have students cut out the three shapes—they will need multiple copies of each one.

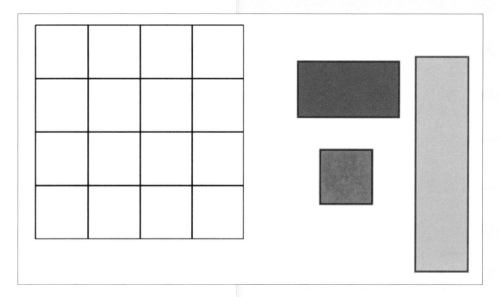

Leading the Activity

- Open the SMART Notebook file you created to display the grid and colored shapes. Ask students to bring their materials and gather in front of the board. Explain that they will use the small colored squares and rectangles to create a fractional part of the large square. Point out that there may be more than one way to achieve that fractional value using those shapes and that they may need to rotate the shapes to fit them together in the desired way.

- Demonstrate how to rotate a shape: Tap a shape, drag it away from the original, and tap it again. A blue frame appears around it. Press the rotate button (green handle) at the top of the frame, and drag it in the direction you want the shape to rotate.

- Pose a question to your students, such as: "What is one way to show me one-fourth of the big square?"

▶ Check It Out!

Go to **http://bit.ly/XaDCAm** (case sensitive) where I'll talk you through how to lead this activity.

Think of the Possibilities

Stretch this activity to have students practice comparing fractions and writing equations to match those comparisons. For example, if students first fill two-eighths of the large square and then fill three-fourths of it, ask them to determine the relationship between the two fractions and write an expression to show the relationship, such as 2/8 < ¾.

◆ Allow students time to figure this with the manipulatives. Then ask for a volunteer to come to the board and position the colored shapes on the big square to show that particular fraction of the square.

◆ While the student at the board is working, ask those on the floor to show you one way to make the desired fraction, helping them if needed. Once the student at the board thinks she's got it, check her work and help her correct it if necessary. In the cases where there is more than one way to make a particular fraction, ask for other volunteers to do just that as time allows.

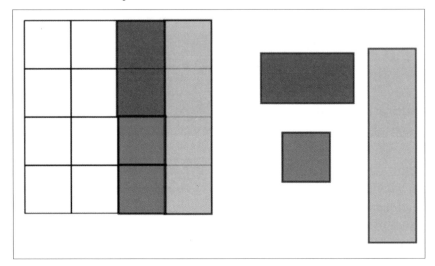

◆ Repeat the process above with other fractions, such as one-half, two-eighths, and three-fourths. When possible, make connections with or for your students about equivalent fractions—one-fourth and two-eighths, for example.

◆ When you're through, close the file by tapping on the x in the upper right corner of the screen. Tap on *No* in the pop-up window.

Building the *Fraction Makers* Page

▶ Check It Out!

Go to **http://bit.ly/Zr6TbM** (case sensitive) where I'll talk you through how to build this SMART Notebook page step by step.

1. Open a new SMART Notebook file by double-clicking on the SMART Notebook icon on your desktop.

2. Click on the *Gallery* tab. Type "squares" in the search box, then click the magnifying glass to the right of the search box. Click on the blue bar titled *Pictures* to view all of the pictures that relate to squares.

3. The first thumbnail image at the top of the tab should be labeled Squares - tessellation. Believe it or not, that's the one you want! Double-click or drag and drop to import the picture of the grid onto your page.

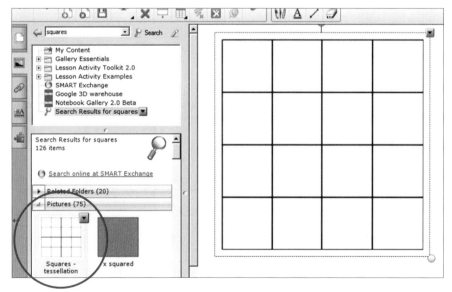

Building the *Fraction Makers* Page *continued*

4. Next, click on the *Shapes* tool in your toolbar. Shape options will appear in the toolbar. You'll be using two different shapes: the square and the rectangle. Click on the square button; then choose a fill color.

Shapes

5. Don't move your cursor down onto the page quite yet. First, you're going to change the *transparency* of the square. It's like magic and super easy to do. Click on the *Transparency* tool, and slide the tab to the right a couple of notches.

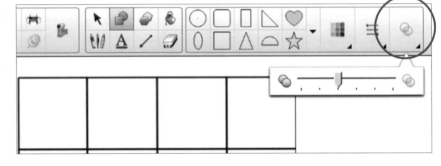

6. Now bring your cursor onto the page (it will appear as crosshairs). Click and drag to make a square the same size as one of the squares in the tessellation grid. The transparency of the square makes this easier because you can see through to match it up with the grid square underneath.

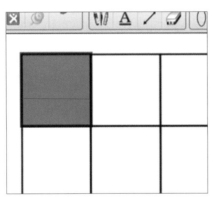

7. Repeat Steps 4 through 6, but choose the rectangle shape. Make one rectangle that is the equivalent of two squares. Then make a second rectangle that is equivalent in size to four tessellation squares. It doesn't matter where you place the rectangles on the tessellation grid; you're just using the grid as a size guide.

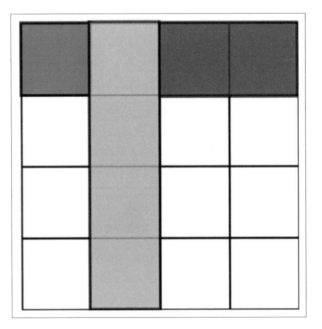

8. Drag each shape to any free space on the page. Here, you'll apply the *Infinite Cloner* function to all three at once. To do so, bring your cursor to the upper left of the shapes and click and drag across them all until a blue frame appears around each one. Click on the gray menu arrow in the upper right corner of one of the frames. Select the *Infinite Cloner* option in the drop-down menu. Applying this function will allow you and your students to endlessly tap and drag copies of each of these shapes around the page.

9. Your page is ready to use! Name and save the file.

Clone	Ctrl+D
Cut	Ctrl+X
Copy	Ctrl+C
Paste	Ctrl+V
Delete	Del
Check Spelling…	
Locking	▶
Grouping	▶
Flip	▶
Order	▶
Infinite Cloner	
Link…	
Sound…	
Properties…	

SMART Tip

You can alter the transparency of any object on a SMART Notebook page, including images and items you've imported from the *Gallery* or text.

SMART Tools and Techniques

Importing and locking an image and creating "hidden" labels

Working with the *Lines*, *Shapes*, *Color*, and *Text* tools

Inside the Human Body

During this SMART Board activity, your students will see themselves from a different perspective (the inside!) while learning the locations of their vital organs. It will also acquaint them with terms related to the human body and provide visuals of what those organs look like. This is a wonderful way to set up a lesson on the human body. This type of SMART Board activity works well for practicing with any material that involves applying labels to diagrams or photos appropriately.

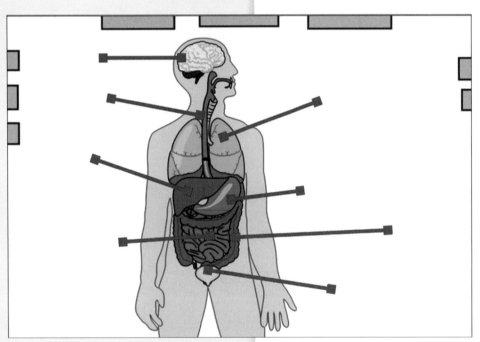

Materials
• Photocopies of the activity page, 1 for each student
• Scissors
• Glue

Before You Begin

Create your own customized version of this activity page following the instructions beginning on page 124. Before making copies, open the SMART Notebook file on your computer and use your mouse to pull the labels on the activity page into view. Print a master copy and then close the file without saving the changes. Make and distribute the photocopies along with the scissors and glue, and ask students to cut out the labels.

▶ **Check It Out!**
Go to **http://bit.ly/Z6Y73j** (case sensitive) where I'll talk you through how to lead this activity.

Leading the Activity

◆ Open the SMART Notebook file you created to display the image your class will be labeling. Ask students to tell you terms they know that might be used to label different parts of the diagram.

◆ Ask one student at a time to come up to the board, pull a tab in from the side, and read the term on it. Help each one read the term if necessary.

◆ Ask the rest of your students to orally direct the child at the board to help him place the label in the correct spot.

◆ Corroborate that the label is placed correctly. Then ask students to paste that label on the correct spot on their diagram.

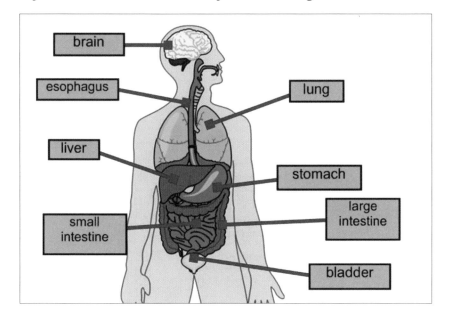

◆ Repeat the exercise, calling up a different volunteer each time, until every tab has been pulled.

◆ When you're through, close the file by tapping on the x in the upper right corner of the screen. Tap on *No* in the pop-up window.

Think of the Possibilities

To provide extra challenge, do not create labels in the SMART Notebook file. Instead, ask students to pick one organ and use a *Pen* tool to write the name of the organ in the correct spot on the board.

You can also create a second set of tabs that describe the job each organ performs (in very simple terms); ask students to first label the organs and then also pair each organ with its function. And, of course, you can change the diagram and labels completely to study the inner workings of a different organism, such as a plant or a fish.

Here's another possibility, this time for social studies: Create a page showing a map, and have your students label it.

Building the *Inside the Human Body* Page

▶ Check It Out!

Go to **http://bit.ly/YdNedJ** (case sensitive) where I'll talk you through how to build this SMART Notebook page step by step.

1. Open a new SMART Notebook file by double-clicking on the SMART Notebook icon on your desktop.

2. Click on the *Gallery* tab. In the search box, type a phrase related to whatever content you plan to study. If you want to create a page like my example, type "inside the body." Click on the magnifying glass that is just to the right of the search box. The results of your search will appear near the middle of the tab in the form of blue bars. Click on the blue bar that says *Pictures*. For this example, choose the *Inside the body* image.

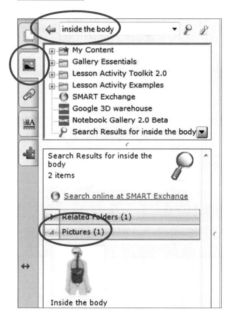

3. Double-click on the image or drag and drop it onto the page. Click, drag, and drop it into position. If needed, click on the image again so that a blue frame appears around it. Then click on the gray menu arrow in the upper right corner and choose *Locking* and then *Lock In Place*. This will prevent the body image from being accidentally moved out of position when students are moving the labels. We certainly don't want the intestines to end up where the brain should be!

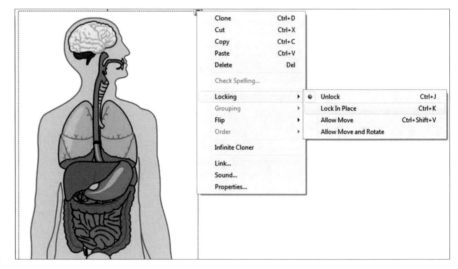

4. Now it's time to create the lines to indicate each organ that can be labeled. Click on the *Lines* tool; a menu of line color and style options will open.

5. Click on the blue line with blocks at both ends to select it. When you move your cursor onto your page, it will turn into crosshairs. Bring your cursor to the first organ you want to label, and click and drag a line out from that organ. When the line is the right length (don't forget to leave room for the label), simply release your mouse.

6. Repeat this process for all of the organs to be labeled. These label lines need to be locked too. Position your cursor near the top left corner of the page, and click and drag it across the page until all the lines are selected. Click on the gray menu arrow of one frame, and choose the *Locking* option and then *Lock In Place*.

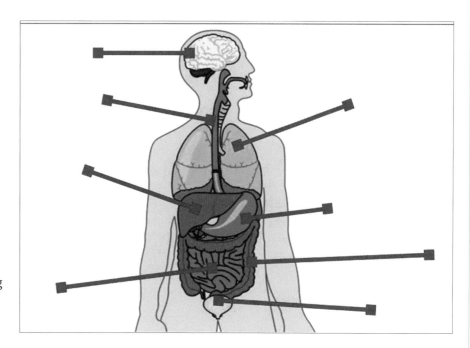

SMART Tip

If you ever want to change the look of one of your lines, click on the **Select** tool, then click on the line you want to change. You can change its length, direction, even its style and color.

Building the *Inside the Human Body* Page *continued*

7. To create the labels, you'll first use the *Shapes* tool. When you click on the *Shapes* tool, shape options will appear in the toolbar. For this example, click on the rectangle. Then click on the *Color* tool and choose the fill color you like.

Shapes

8. Move your cursor onto the page; it will turn to crosshairs. Click and drag your cursor to make a rectangle; repeat for each label. Keep in mind the length of the word you'll be typing into each rectangle and size it accordingly. To keep the page logically arranged, place one rectangle next to each label line you made in Step 5. You don't want to forget any vital organs!

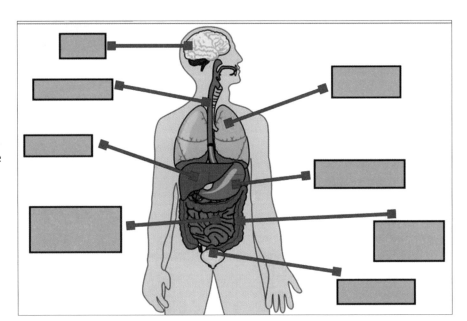

9. Next, you'll add the text of the labels. Click on the *Select* tool in your toolbar, and then double-click inside one of the rectangles. Text options will appear in your toolbar. Choose center-justify and then the font and font size. Type in the label. Do leave a little extra space at each end of the word (you'll need it in the next step).

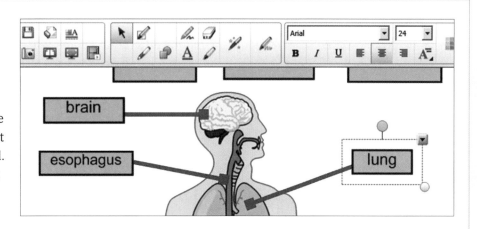

10. Repeat the process for each label (you may need to adjust font size for some labels). If you want to adjust the size of a rectangle a bit once the text is inside, double-click on it again. A white bubble will appear on each side of the box, and a gray button will appear in the lower corner of the box. Click on any of these and drag to tweak the sizing. The text inside will readjust itself to fit.

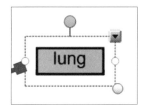

11. Now you need to move each rectangle to any page edge until only a small portion of the rectangle shows—just enough to tap and drag back out. Do this by clicking on the rectangle, dragging it over to the edge until it has almost disappeared, and dropping it. Such a cool but simple trick!

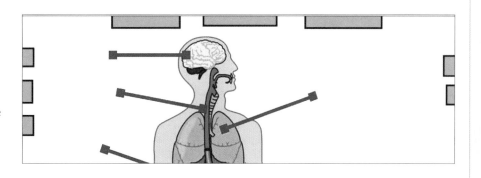

12. Your diagram is ready to roll! Be sure to name and save the file.

SMART Tools and Techniques

Importing and resizing objects and using the *Infinite Cloner* and *Dual Page Display* techniques

Working with the *Page Sorter* tab

Combination Contemplation

Creating different combinations out of a set of objects is an engaging critical thinking exercise. It's also the type of exercise that frequently shows up on standardized assessments. This activity is designed to get students thinking about the process of creating combinations using something they are very familiar with—clothes!

Materials

- Photocopies of the activity page, 1 for each group, cut apart

Before You Begin

Create your own customized version of this activity page following the instructions beginning on page 130.

▶ **Check It Out!**
Go to **http://bit.ly/XLP60Z** (case sensitive) where I'll talk you through how to lead this activity.

Leading the Activity

◆ Open the SMART Notebook file you created to display the clothing images. Then click on page 2 of the activity in the *Page Sorter* tab to show both pages at once.

◆ Divide students into groups of four, and give each group a set of the clothing images. Ask groups to sit together in front of the SMART Board.

◆ Tell your students that you're going to challenge them to come up with as many combinations of clothing as possible. Each combination must contain one top, one bottom, and one pair of shoes. (The outfits don't have to match!) For each unique combination a team creates, the team will earn 1 point.

◆ Ask a member of Team One to come to the board and create an outfit by dragging items of clothing to the blank page. If the student is successful, award Team One a point on your tally sheet (or dry-erase board).

- Invite Team Two to send up a member to create a different outfit. Explain to the students that in between their official turns at the board, they may quietly confer with their teammates to come up with a new combination in preparation for their turn.

- Continue the activity until all teams have had a turn. Then begin again with Team One. Ideally, each time a team's turn comes around, a different member of that team will use the SMART Board. If a team cannot think of a new combination, they need to pass to the next team. Be sure to continue keeping score on your tally sheet!

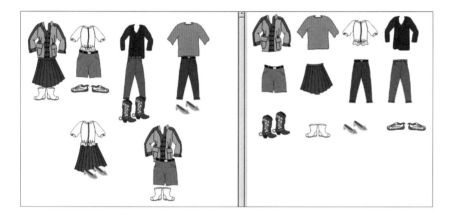

- The game ends when all possible combinations have been made. The team with the most points wins.

- When you're through, close the file by tapping on the x in the upper right corner of the screen. Tap on *No* in the pop-up window.

Think of the Possibilities

You'll get plenty of mileage out this page simply by switching in other sets of objects that are right up your students' alley—think pizza or hamburger toppings, for instance. You can also bring letters or numbers into the mix and challenge students to figure out how many different ways they can be arranged.

SMART Tip

To get out of dual page display view, tap the same button in your toolbar that got

you there to begin with—*View Screens*. Among the options in the drop-down menu, look for *Single Page Display*. Tap it, and the screen will snap back to a single page view.

Building the *Combination Contemplation* Page

ⓞ Check It Out!

Go to **http://bit.ly/Zr72vU** (case sensitive) where I'll talk you through how to build this SMART Notebook page step by step.

1. Open a new SMART Notebook file by double-clicking on the SMART Notebook icon on your desktop.

2. Open the *Gallery* tab and type "clothes" in the search box. Then click on the magnifying glass to the right of the search box. Once the search results appear, click on the blue bar entitled *Pictures*.

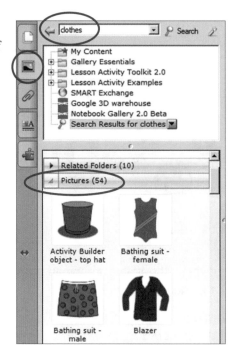

3. Scroll down through the images and drag and drop (or double-click) any that you want to use onto your page. Aim for three or more choices of each category of clothing (tops, bottoms, hats, and so on) you decide to include. If you work with younger students, you might want to start with two of each item.

4. After you finish selecting items, you'll need to size them so they all fit comfortably on the page. Click on an image and a blue frame appears around it. Click and hold the gray resize button in the lower right corner of the frame, and drag your mouse in or out until the object is the size you want.

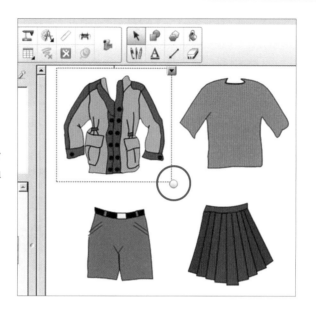

5. Next you'll need to clone the images. You can do this all in one fell swoop. Click in the upper left corner of your page and drag your mouse across the images until they all have blue frames around them. Click on just one gray menu arrow in the upper right corner of one image and select *Infinite Cloner*. Now all of those items selected can be repeatedly dragged and dropped elsewhere on the screen as often as needed.

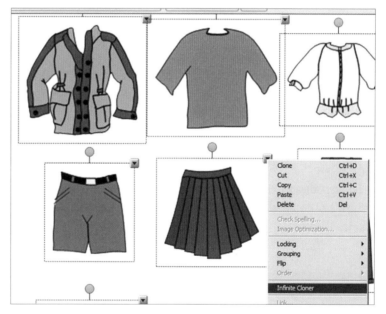

6. At this stage, you need to add a second, blank page to this activity. This is as simple as it gets. Click the *Add Page* button in your toolbar and a blank page will appear on your screen and in the *Page Sorter* tab. Easy, right?

Building the *Combination Contemplation* Page *continued*

7. In order for the activity to work smoothly, this blank page must be moved into the slot *before* the page with the clothing on it. Click on the *Page Sorter* tab (if it's not already open). Click on the thumbnail of the blank page, drag your cursor up above the thumbnail of the page with the clothing on it, and then release your mouse. The blank page should now be page 1 and the one with the images has become page 2.

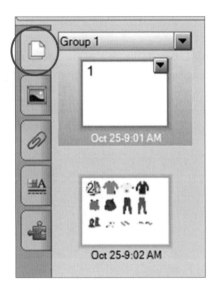

8. Next, you'll create the split-screen effect. In the *Page Sorter* tab, click on page 2; a blue frame appears around it. In your toolbar at the top of the page, click on the *View Screens* tool. Choose the option titled *Dual Page Display*. Now your screen should show both pages side by side.

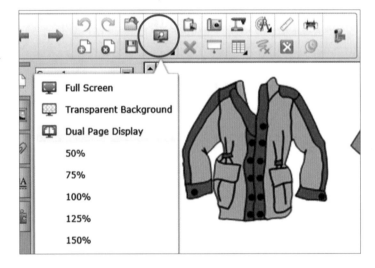

9. Name and save the file. When you open it up to use with your students, all you'll have to do is click on the thumbnail of page 2 in the *Page Sorter* tab, and you'll be ready to go.

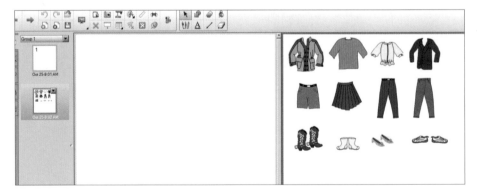

Sentence Detectives

Understanding sentence structure is a key to strong reading comprehension and clearer writing, so why not practice it with your students at the SMART Board? This activity gives students a lively opportunity to use their voices while building critical thinking skills as they "fix" sentences that have structural flaws. You'll be able to adapt this page format for practicing math facts and improving reading fluency and comprehension too. Your students will love the reveal feature of this activity—guaranteed!

Materials
- Individual dry-erase boards
- Dry-erase markers

Before You Begin

Create your own customized version of this activity page following the instructions beginning on page 135. Distribute the dry-erase boards and markers to your students.

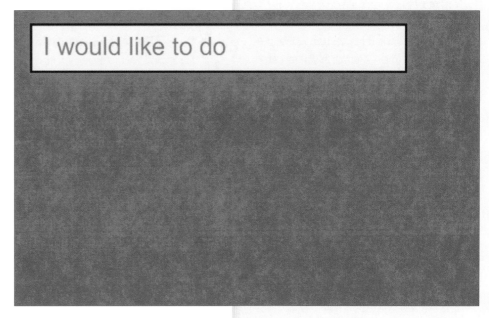

SMART Tools and Techniques

Using the ordering, locking, and background fill techniques for a "magic reveal" effect

Working with the *Text*, *Shapes*, *Color*, and *Clear Ink* tools

▶ **Check It Out!**

Go to **http://bit.ly/YbRayR** (case sensitive) where I'll talk you through how to lead this activity.

Leading the Activity

◆ Open the SMART Notebook file you created to display the yellow rectangle on the orange background. Ask your students to bring their materials and gather in front of the board. Explain that they will be acting as detectives—searching for logical sentences. They'll use two words for responding to your questions: *Huh?* and *Yes!* If you wish, write the words on a flip chart or dry-erase board where students can reference them. Explain that they will use the word *Huh?* when they think a sentence isn't complete (when it makes them say "Huh?" inside their heads). They will use *Yes!* if they think the sentence is complete.

◆ Drag the rectangle until it uncovers a phrase. Ask for a volunteer to read it, or read it to your students if necessary. Ask students to write *Huh?* or *Yes!* on their dry-erase boards, depending on what they think about the phrase. Then, at your signal, ask students to hold their boards up for you to see and/or to say "Huh?" or "Yes!" aloud.

Think of the Possibilities

Use this format to improve reading comprehension by creating complete sentences, including some that simply don't make sense, such as: The young girl ate a sofa for lunch. Ask your students to explain why each sentence is or is not a logical thought.

For math instruction, fill the page with hidden equations instead of sentences with missing phrases. When you reveal an accurate equation, such as $5 + 6 = 7 + 4$, your students will (I hope!) respond with a resounding "Yes!" And when you reveal a false equation, such as 12 inches = 3 feet, you'd want them to say "Huh?" and then come up with some solutions that make the equation true.

SMART Tip

Try using this page, or one like it, as a center. Once students have made the corrections they think necessary on the page, they can print it for you to review later. Demonstrate how to use the *Clear Ink*

Clear Ink

tool to remove the writing they added to the page to leave it ready for the next student.

I would like to do **a puzzle.**

- ◆ If the phrase is a complete sentence, move on to the next phrase by dragging the rectangle down to reveal it.

- ◆ If the phrase does not make a complete thought, ask your students for input. What needs to be added to change the phrase into a complete sentence?

- ◆ Invite a volunteer to come to the board, choose a *Pen* tool, and make the addition or deletion. Or you can ask the students to use their dry-erase boards to write what needs to be added.

- ◆ Tap and drag the yellow rectangle to reveal the next phrase.

- ◆ Repeat this process until all phrases have been reviewed.

- ◆ When you're through, close the file by tapping on the x in the upper right corner of the screen. Tap on *No* in the pop-up window.

Building the *Sentence Detectives* Page

▶ **Check It Out!**
Go to **http://bit.ly/XaJb1B** (case sensitive) where I'll talk you through how to build this SMART Notebook page step by step.

1. Open a new SMART Notebook file by double-clicking on the SMART Notebook icon on your desktop. Write out the phrases or other content you want to use for the activity.

2. Click on the *Text* tool, and text options will appear in your toolbar. Choose the options you like for a font and its color and size. In this case, the color ink you use for the text will also be the background color—that's what makes the reveal effect so cool! I chose orange.

3. Once you've selected your text preferences, click on the page and a text box will appear. Type six phrases, each one on its own line. Make sure that three or four are not complete sentences, and don't give away the complete sentences by adding ending punctuation. It's easier to type all of the content in one text box rather than making a new box for each phrase.

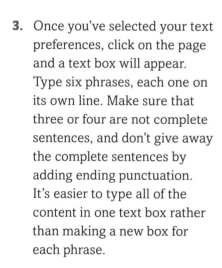

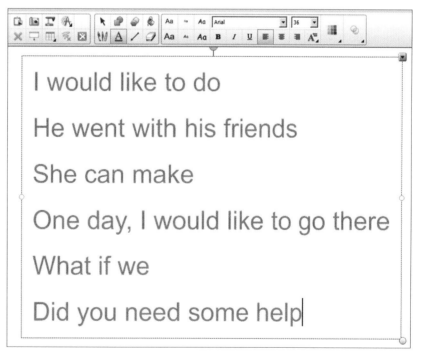

I would like to do

He went with his friends

She can make

One day, I would like to go there

What if we

Did you need some help

Building the *Sentence Detectives* Page *continued*

4. The next step is to lock this text box in place so that it can't be moved by accident when you and your class are engaged in the activity. If needed, click on the text to select it. Click on the gray menu arrow in the upper right corner of the blue frame, and choose *Locking* in the drop-down menu, then choose *Lock In Place.*

I would like to do

He went with his friends

She can make

One day, I would like to go there

Clone	Ctrl+D
Cut	Ctrl+X
Copy	Ctrl+C
Paste	Ctrl+V
Delete	Del

Check Spelling...

Locking		►
• Unlock	Ctrl+J	
Lock In Place	Ctrl+K	
Allow Move	Ctrl+Shift+V	
Allow Move and Rotate		

Grouping	►
Flip	►
Order	►

Infinite Cloner

Link...
Sound...
Properties...

5. Now click on your *Shapes* tool, choose the rectangle, and bring your cursor to the beginning of the longest phrase on your page. Click and drag your cursor across that phrase until it is surrounded by a rectangle. Release your mouse button when you're happy with the size of the rectangle—it doesn't have to precisely match the size of the rectangle in my example page.

Shapes

I would like to do

He went with his friends

She can make

One day, I would like to go there

What if we

Did you need some help

6. The next step is to change the background color of the page to match the ink color you chose. Click on the *Select* tool. Then click somewhere in the white space on the page. Click on your *Properties* tab to open it. You'll see several fill options. Choose *Solid fill* and a color palette will appear. Click on the same color square you chose for your text color. When you do so, all of the text will seem to disappear. Don't worry, it's still there, it's just "under cover" right now! All you should see on the screen is the rectangle in a sea of color.

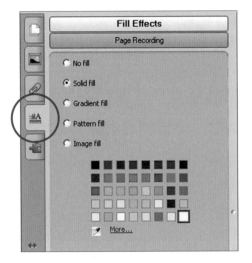

7. At this point, in order to make the reveal effect work, select your rectangle by clicking anywhere on its black outline. Then choose a fill color for it that is different from the background color.

8. SMART Notebook pages have four built-in layers. These layers are part of the "magic" that creates a reveal feature. Your next step will be to move the rectangle into a different layer of the page from the text. Click on the gray menu arrow in the upper right corner of the blue frame around the rectangle, and choose the *Order* option from the dropdown menu and then *Send to Back*.

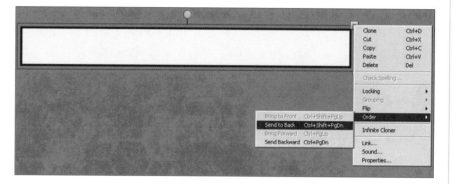

9. Now, the phrase inside the rectangle should have magically reappeared! And as you drag the rectangle from spot to spot on the screen, it should reveal all of the content you typed. Once you've checked that the reveal feature is working correctly, name and save the file.

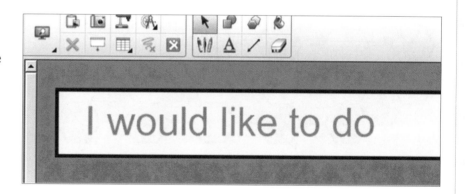

SMART Tip

If you ever want to change the background color of a page, you can simply click on the *Properties* tab and then on *Solid Fill* and choose a new color. With this activity, be sure to change the ink color of the text to match also; otherwise, the reveal feature won't work.

SMART Tools and Techniques

Cloning and locking shapes in place

Working with the *Regular Polygons, Color,* and *Text* tools

Reading Roadway

Use this team game to review the words your students encounter most frequently. Students will learn from one another while they gain additional exposure to these important literary gems and strengthen the Reading Foundational Skills put forth in the Common Core State Standards. This activity is geared toward sight words, but this SMART Notebook format can be adapted to review other language concepts and many math concepts. Once you know how to create this virtual game board, the sky's the limit!

Materials
- A set of number cards from 1 to 6

Before You Begin

Create your own customized version of this activity page following the instructions beginning on page 140.

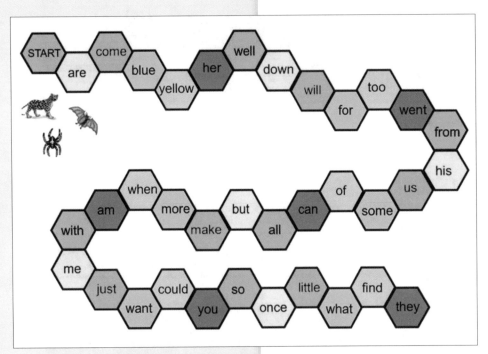

▶ Check It Out!

Go to **http://bit.ly/XzXnXP** (case sensitive) where I'll talk you through how to lead this activity.

Leading the Activity

◆ Open the SMART Notebook file you created to display the roadway; check to be sure all the game pieces are on the START space. Divide your students into two or three teams, and ask them to gather as teams in front of the board.

◆ Assign each team a game piece. Shuffle the set of number cards and place them in a convenient spot (or hold them in your hands).

◆ Ask the first player on Team One to choose a number card and move her team's game piece that number of spaces along the roadway. Then challenge her to read the word printed in the space where the piece landed. If she is successful, congratulate her and explain that she gets to leave her team's game piece on that space. If she cannot read the word, ask her to move the game piece back two spaces.

- To reinforce the learning, ask all Team One members to stand up and read the word together.

- Ask the first player on the next team to choose a card and take a turn.

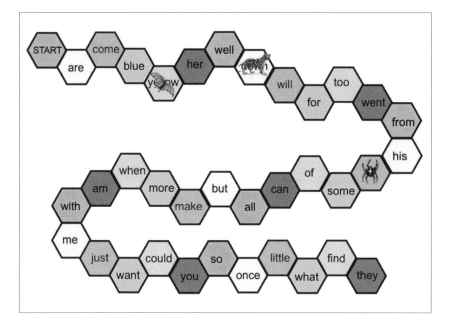

- Play continues until one team's game piece arrives at the last space on the road.

- When you're through, close the file by tapping on the x in the upper right corner of the screen. Tap on *No* in the pop-up window.

Think of the Possibilities

Adapt this game for almost any content your students can recognize on the spot. Instead of placing sight words in the hexagons, you could insert one- to four-digit numbers, letters, shapes, spelling or vocabulary words, color puddles, or coins.

To add another dimension to the activity, ask students to provide more than just the name of the item. For example, with multi-digit numbers, ask students to tell you how many tens there are in the number. If the focus of the exercise is on individual alphabet letters, ask students to make the sound of the letter or state a word that begins with that letter.

SMART Tip

You can print this page and make laminated game boards for students to use in pairs or trios around the room. Provide each group of students a die and an appropriate number of game pieces. Play will be nearly the same: If a student can read the word, he can stay on the spot he landed on. If he cannot read the word, then his group mates can help him but he will have to move back two spaces.

Building the *Reading Roadway* Page

▶ Check It Out!

Go to **http://bit.ly/Z1ZFIU** (case sensitive) where I'll talk you through how to build this SMART Notebook page step by step.

1. Open a new SMART Notebook file by double-clicking on the SMART Notebook icon on your desktop. Jot down the sight words (or other content) you will use to fill in the roadway you'll be creating.

2. Click on the *Regular Polygons* button in your toolbar. A set of additional tool buttons will appear with options for number of sides, color, and other features.

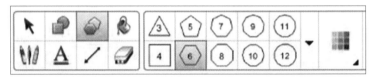

3. Click on the six-sided polygon to select it, and then click on the *Color* button. Click on the fill color of your choice from the color palette.

4. Move your cursor onto the blank page. It will change appearance, becoming crosshairs. Click and drag your mouse until you've made a hexagon about the size of a quarter, then release.

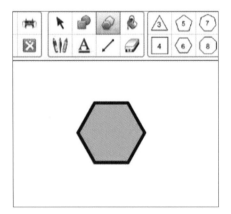

SMART Tip

To reverse the *Infinite Cloner* option, click on the shape and then click on the menu arrow that appears in the upper right corner of the blue frame. You'll see the words *Infinite Cloner* with a check mark next to them. Click the check mark and it will disappear. Now you will no longer be able to clone the object until you reselect that option.

5. Click on the *Select* button, and then click and drag the hexagon to the place on the page where you want the game track to start. (A corner of the page is best.) Click on the shape to select it, and a frame will appear around it. Click on the gray menu arrow in the upper right corner of the frame. Click on *Infinite Cloner* in the drop-down menu.

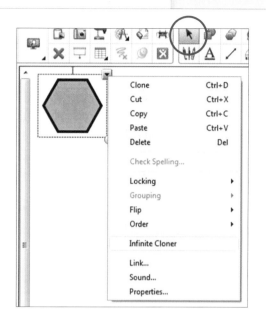

6. Now your mouse has acquired special power! You can create as many hexagons as you wish simply by clicking on the original hexagon (a hexagon clone will then appear) and dragging the clone to another spot on the page. Link each hexagon to the previous one by joining them on one side. Make your roadway as long and winding as you'd like. Note that you must click on your *original* hexagon each time you want to make a new clone. You can't clone a clone!

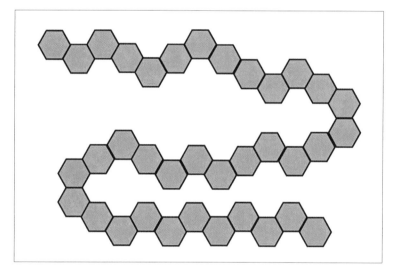

7. To change the color of a hexagon, start by clicking on it. A blue frame will appear around the hexagon and the *Color* tool button will reappear at the top of the screen. Click on the button and then click on the specific color you want that hexagon to be.

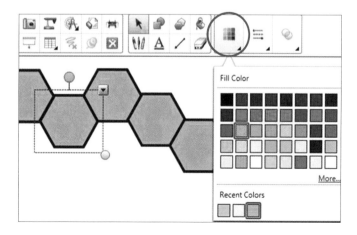

Building the *Reading Roadway* Page *continued*

8. Repeat this sequence for each hexagon you want to change.

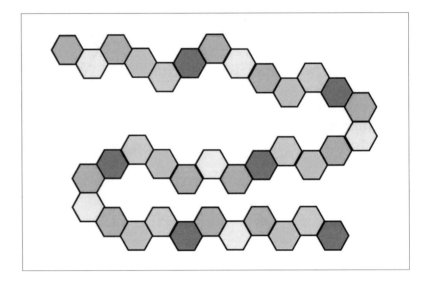

9. Now it's time to get words into those boxes. The easiest way to do this is to click on the *Text* button. Additional tool buttons will appear.

10. Choose the font and font size you want in the options menu, or simply use the default settings. Click on the first hexagon of your roadway. Type the word "START."

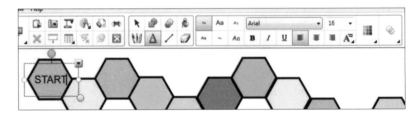

SMART Tip

The "roadway" format is useful for many kinds of activities. I recommend saving a basic version in the *Gallery* so that you can access it anytime and add new content. Once you've finished Step 8, name the file something like Basic Roadway and save it. Then right-click on the thumbnail of that page in the *Page Sorter* tab, and select *Add Page to Gallery* from the drop-down menu. A copy of the page will be moved to a section of the *Gallery* called *My Content*.

In the future (as long as you are using the same computer on which you created the page) you can open your *My Content* folder, add this page to any file you have open, and then add content in each hexagon and lock the roadway in place. This trick saves a ton of time!

11. Click on the next hexagon, and type the first sight word from your list. Repeat this process for the rest of the hexagons. If a text box doesn't quite line up the way you want inside a hexagon, just click the *Select* tool (the *Text* tool buttons will disappear) and then click and drag the word to adjust its placement.

12. At this point it is smart (no pun intended!) to lock your roadway in place. That way, when students move the game pieces, the hexagons and words will stay fixed in place. To do this, bring your cursor to the upper left corner of the page and click and drag across the entire page until every element has a blue frame around it.

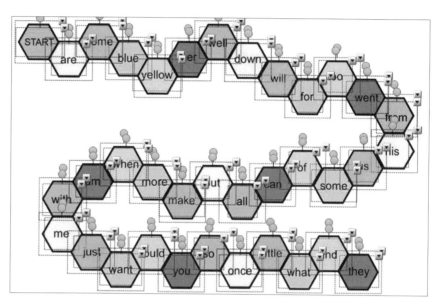

13. Click on any gray menu arrow anywhere on the page. In the drop-down menu, click on the *Locking* option, then select *Lock In Place*. This one step locks every selected item in place.

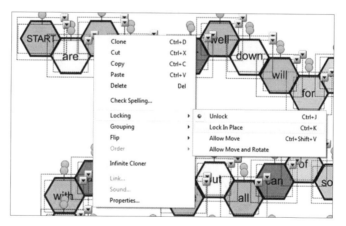

Building the *Reading Roadway* Page *continued*

14. The next task is to make the game pieces, and here your creativity can take free rein. You can choose pictures from the *Gallery* of animals, import images of race cars from the Internet, or use simple shapes (if you browse for images on the Internet, be sure to avoid copyrighted images). Let's go to the *Gallery* and find some animals. Click on the *Gallery* tab and type "animals" in the search box, and click on the magnifying glass icon next to the box.

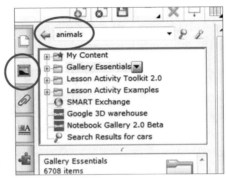

15. When the search results appear, click on the blue bar titled *Pictures* and scroll down to view all the pictures. Choose an animal you like and drag and drop it onto your game board. When you release the cursor, a blue frame will appear around the animal. Position your cursor over the gray resize button in the lower right corner of the frame and move your mouse until the image is the size you want. Then click anywhere on the screen to release the image. (Hint: It should be about the same size as your hexagons.)

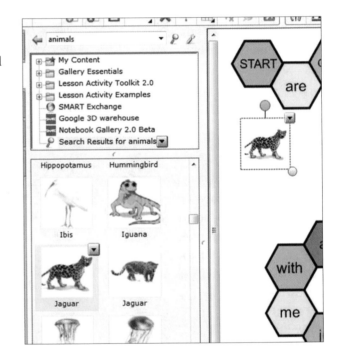

16. Repeat Step 15 to add one or two more animals to your page—depending on how many teams you'll have.

17. Save and name the file. You're ready to go!

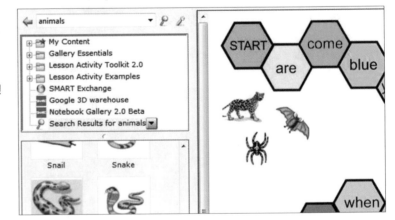

Coffee Can Sentences

Sentence building is more fun when your students can pluck sentence sections from a can, rotate them, flip them, read them, and vote on them. This activity brings the touch technology of your SMART Board to the forefront and has a natural, easy interactive component for everyone. The bonus here is that this activity also works as a center with students interacting with the SMART Board itself or using paper counterparts and a little glue.

Materials
- Paper plates
- Markers

Before You Begin
Create your own customized version of this activity page following the instructions beginning on page 147. Distribute the paper plates and markers, and ask students to draw a smiley face on one side and a sad face on the other.

SMART Tools and Techniques

Cloning, grouping, ordering, and rotating shapes and text

Working with the *Shapes, Text,* and *Color* tools

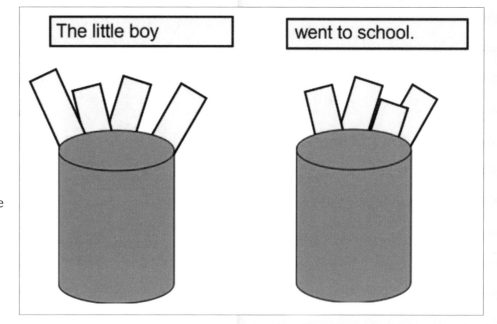

The little boy

went to school.

Leading the Activity

◆ Open the SMART Notebook file you created to display the two coffee cans. Ask students to bring their plates and gather in front of the board. Explain that they will have three jobs: (1) creating sentences using phrases shown on the board, (2) voting on whether the sentences created on the board are correct or not, and (3) brainstorming words or phrases that would create complete sentences.

◆ Ask for a volunteer to come to the SMART Board and drag out one virtual slip of paper from each can on the board.

◆ It may be necessary for the slips to be rotated so they can be read. Show your students how to do this. (Tap a slip of paper so that a frame appears around it. Tap the green rotate handle at the top of the frame, and drag your finger clockwise or counterclockwise to orient the slip correctly.)

▶ Check It Out!
Go to **http://bit.ly/Ytx6qX** (case sensitive) where I'll talk you through how to lead this activity.

Think of the Possibilities

Sentence building is just one option for this activity. The virtual slips of paper in the cans can be created for pairing up math expressions and answers, words that rhyme, states and capitals, English and Spanish word pairs, and so on.

To make the sentence building more challenging, add a third can and have students draw three slips each time instead of just two.

◆ Ask whether the student thinks she can arrange the phrases in some order to make a complete sentence. If the student says yes, tell her to go ahead and make the sentence. Then ask her classmates to vote by holding up their plates. Showing a smiley face means "I agree with your sentence." Showing a sad face means "I don't agree" or "I'm not sure."

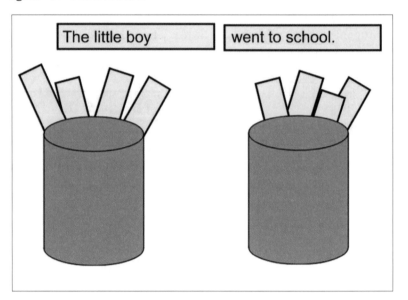

The little boy   went to school.

◆ Guide students to the correct answer. If the student was successful, ask her to drag the phrases back into the cans.

◆ If a sentence cannot be built by pairing the two phrases, ask students to brainstorm words or phrases that would make at least one part of the pair a complete sentence. Then drag the phrases back into the cans.

◆ Continue the activity, inviting a different student to the board each round.

◆ When you're through, close the file by tapping on the x in the upper right corner of the screen. Tap on *No* in the pop-up window.

Building the *Coffee Can Sentences* Page

▶ Check It Out!
Go to **http://bit.ly/WKd1z2** (case sensitive) where I'll talk you through how to build this SMART Notebook page step by step.

1. Open a new SMART Notebook file by double-clicking on the SMART Notebook icon on your desktop. Write out the sentences or other content you want to use for the activity.

2. Open the *Gallery* tab and type "cylinder" in the search box. Click on the magnifying glass just to the right of the search box. Click on the blue *Pictures* bar and scroll down until you see the picture of a blue cylinder. Double-click that cylinder to import it onto your page.

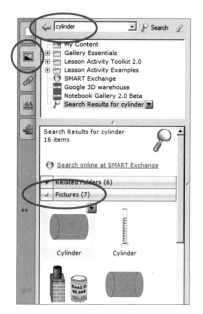

3. While the cylinder on your page still has the blue frame around it, click on the gray resize button in the lower right corner of that blue frame and drag it in or out to size the cylinder. Click on the green rotate handle at the top of that blue frame, and drag your mouse until the cylinder is upright.

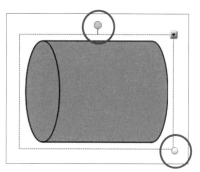

Building the *Coffee Can Sentences* Page *continued*

4. Now you'll create the virtual slips of paper. Click on the *Shapes* tool and choose the rectangle from the shapes menu. Click on the *Color* button and choose a fill color.

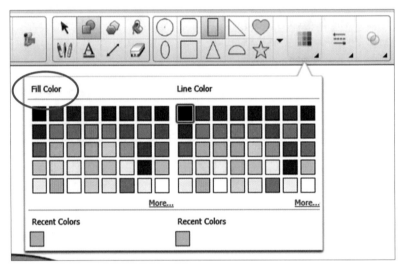

5. Move your cursor to the page, and click and drag to create a rectangle that is a bit longer than the cylinder is tall. Then click on the *Select* tool. Click on the gray menu arrow in the upper right corner of the blue frame, and choose the *Infinite Cloner* option. This will allow you to endlessly generate new rectangles from the original.

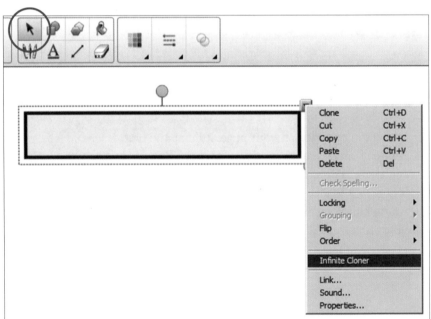

SMART Tip

When you click on the *Shape*s tool, you'll see approximately 10 choices. But if you click on the little black arrow immediately to the right of those choices, you'll see a whole bunch more!

6. Drag five or six rectangles off from the original; position them so that none overlap. Click on the *Text* tool, and then click on one of the rectangles. On your sheet of composed text, divide each sentence and phrase approximately in half. Then, on your computer, type the first half of the sentence or phrase inside the rectangle.

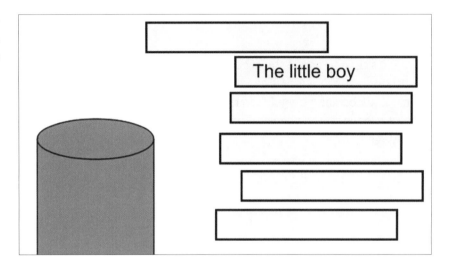

7. Now you can rotate the rectangle using the green rotate handle (like you did with the cylinder in Step 3) and slip the sentence strip into the can. When you try this, if the slip remains in front of the can, you'll need to change the layer of the page that the can is in. This is simple. Select the can and click on the gray menu arrow in the corner of the blue frame. In the drop-down menu, choose *Order*, then *Bring to Front*. Now all your slips of paper should appear to "slide" into the can, and the words on them will be hidden from view.

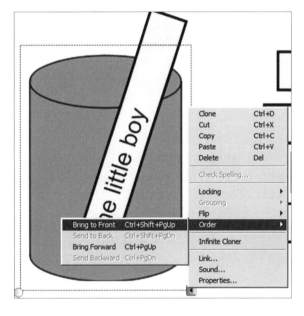

Building the *Coffee Can Sentences* Page *continued*

8. Add text for the first half of the rest of the sentences and phrases to each of the remaining rectangles, and insert them into the can, just as you did the first one.

9. Now it's time to create the second can and its contents. Clone your first can by right-clicking on it and choosing *Copy*. Then right-click in the empty space on the page and paste the can onto the page.

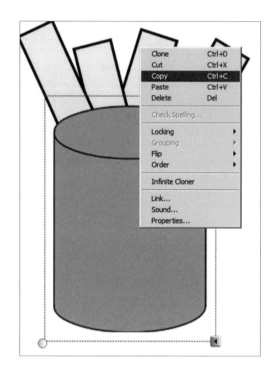

10. This is a good time to lock those cans in place so that when your students are moving the slips of paper in and out, the cans don't get moved by mistake. Right-click on one, open the drop-down menu, and choose *Locking*, then *Lock In Place*. Repeat for the other can.

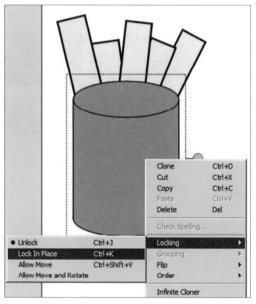

11. Now it's just a repeat of creating the rectangles and adding text to each one. Make sure that each slip of paper in the first can has a mate in the second can!

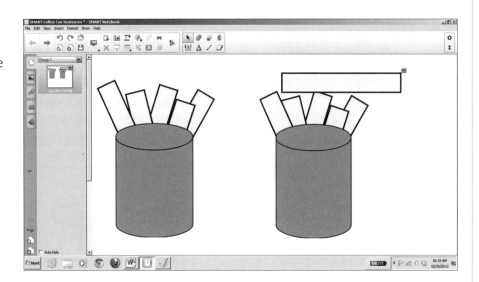

12. Unless you are overly attached to your original rectangle, it's a good idea to delete it so that it's not in the way when your students are doing the activity. Right-click on it, and then click on the little check mark that appears next to the words *Infinite Cloner*.

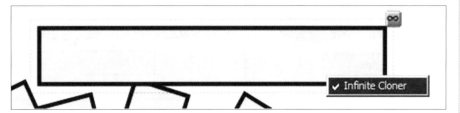

13. Open the drop-down menu for the rectangle and choose *Delete*. Whew! Your page is ready to go. Be sure to name and save the file.

SMART Tools and Techniques

Grouping, ordering, and cloning text and shapes

Working with the *Lines, Shapes,* and *Text* tools

Contraction Cover-Up

Use a little SMART Board magic as you review word pairs that make up common contractions. This activity works well in a whole-group format as described below, but it's also designed to be self-checking so that students can use it on their own or in pairs during centers or anchor activities. This kind of cover-up activity also works well for other types of language practice and for math facts practice too. Your SMART Board is so versatile!

Materials
- Dry-erase boards, 1 for each student
- Dry-erase markers

Before You Begin

Create your own customized version of this activity page following the instructions beginning on page 154. Distribute the dry-erase boards and markers to your students.

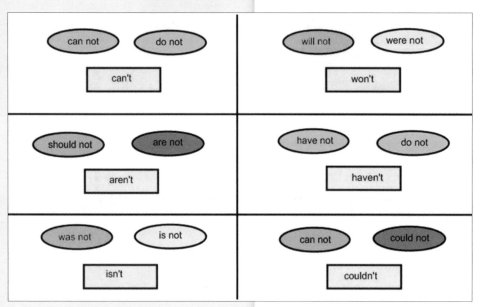

▶ Check It Out!

Go to **http://bit.ly/Z1WeSk** (case sensitive) where I'll talk you through how to lead this activity.

Leading the Activity

◆ Open the SMART Notebook file you created to display the word pairs and contractions. Ask students to bring their materials and gather in front of the board. Explain that their job will be to decide which pair of words is the right one to form the corresponding contraction.

◆ Ask for a volunteer to come to the board. Direct him to drag one contraction to cover up the word pair he thinks makes up that contraction.

◆ Ask students who are not at the board to write the word pair they think is correct on their dry-erase boards and hold them up for you to check.

◆ Once the student at the board completes the action, explain the result: If he chose the correct word pair, the contraction has covered up the oval containing those words. If he chose the wrong word pair, the contraction has disappeared behind the oval.

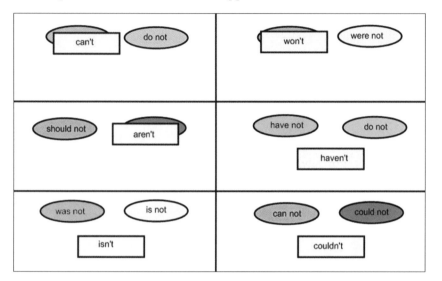

◆ Repeat the exercise, inviting a different volunteer to the board each time.

◆ When you're through, close the file by tapping on the x in the upper right corner of the screen. Tap on *No* in the pop-up window.

Think of the Possibilities

Cover-up activities are conducive to practicing many kinds of content, so I hope your brain is juicing! For example, if your students are practicing math facts, set up a display of math expressions and answers and ask students to move the expression up to the correct answer. (If it's correct, the expression will cover up the answer.)

If rhyming words are on tap, students can move the word in the rectangle to match a rhyming word in an oval. If they choose the correct word, the rectangle will cover up the oval.

You can also practice syllabication in this format. Students determine the number of syllables in the word in the rectangle and then drag the rectangle up to a word that has the same number of syllables. If they are correct, the rectangle will cover up the word.

Building the *Contraction Cover-Up* Page

▶ Check It Out!

Go to **http://bit.ly/Z1ZKMC** (case sensitive) where I'll talk you through how to build this SMART Notebook page step by step.

1. Open a new SMART Notebook file by double-clicking on the SMART Notebook icon on your desktop. Jot down the contractions and word pairs (or other content) you'll be using on this page.

2. Click on the *Lines* tool in the toolbar at the top of your page. Select the solid line option.

3. Decide how many sections you want on the page. (I created six sections on my example page.) Move the cursor (which will now look like crosshairs) to the top middle of the page, and click and drag your cursor down the center of the page to divide it in half vertically.

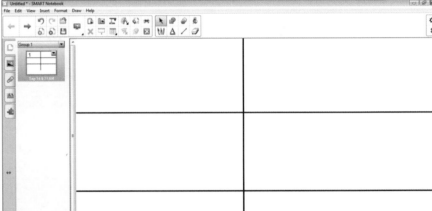

4. Repeat this action twice from left to right to make horizontal lines. You'll end up with six approximately equal sections on the page. If your lines are not quite where you want them, don't worry. Choose the *Select* tool and then click on the line you want to move. Drag it left or right or up or down until it's in the right spot.

5. Now it's time to choose the two shapes you want. I used a rectangle and an oval, but other shapes would work well too. Click on the *Shapes* tool and additional buttons will appear in the toolbar. Click on the rectangle button and then the *Color* button. In the color palette, click on the color of your choice (this will be the fill color for the rectangle). Bring your cursor onto one section of your page. Click and drag the cursor until the rectangle is the size you want. Repeat this process to make a colored oval.

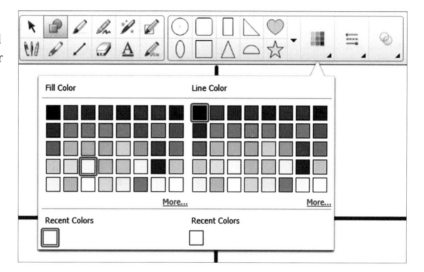

6. Click on the *Select* tool and then the oval; a blue frame will appear around it. Now click on the gray menu arrow in the upper right corner of the frame. In the dropdown menu, choose the *Clone* option. A second, identical oval will appear, and it should have a blue frame around it. Click and drag it into place next to the original oval. If you want to change the color of your second oval, click on the *Color* button again to bring up the color palette, and choose a color.

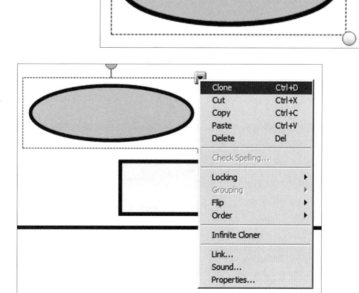

Building the *Contraction Cover-Up* Page *continued*

7. Your next task is to layer the shapes in a particular order (front to back) on the page. Every SMART Notebook page has four layers to it. You'll place shapes in two of those layers: This will allow some shapes to cover up other shapes. First, click on the rectangle to select it. Click on the gray menu arrow and choose the *Order* option in the drop-down menu, and then *Bring to Front*. Repeat this with *one* of your ovals.

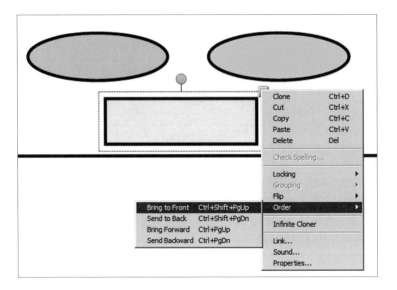

8. Select the othere oval. Choose the *Order* option from the drop-down menu again, but this time choose *Send to Back*.

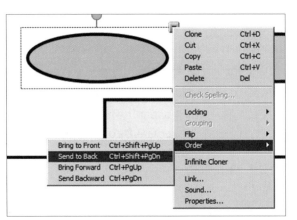

9. Now that your shapes are layered, it's time to make a copy of them for each section of the page. Click somewhere to the upper left of the three shapes and drag your cursor across until all three are bordered by blue frames. Click on the gray menu arrow on one frame and select *Copy* in the drop-down menu.

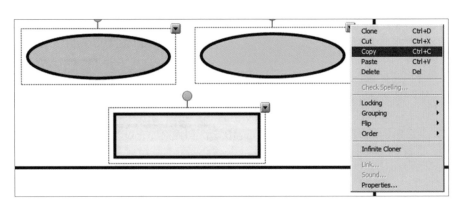

10. Next, place your cursor in one empty section of the page, right-click, and select *Paste*. Repeat this pasting step for each section of your page. These copied shapes will already have been assigned to the correct layer of the page, so you don't need to "order" them.

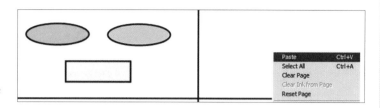

11. Now you'll place text in each of your shapes. In each rectangle, you will type a contraction. Click on the *Text* tool in your toolbar and then on a rectangle. A text box will appear. In the toolbar, you will also see options for font and its size and color. You can change the look of the text as you like. Type the contraction "can't." If the word doesn't end up directly in the center of the rectangle, click on the *Select* tool (if necessary) and move the text or the shape as needed.

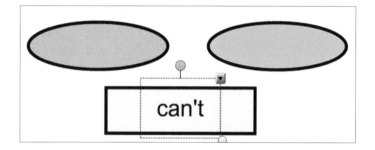

12. The next task is to group the text with the rectangle itself; this ensures that the text and shape will remain a unit as they're dragged around the board. If you didn't click on *Select* in the last step, do so now. Then click on the white space outside the shape and drag your mouse across it until both the shape and the text are framed. Click on a gray menu arrow and choose *Grouping* and then *Group*. Now the text and the shape are "glued" together.

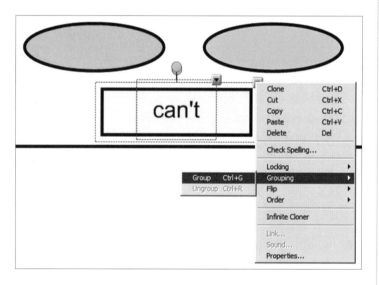

SMART Tip

To unglue items you've grouped together, select the group of items and then click on the gray menu arrow to open the drop-down menu. Click on *Grouping* and then *Ungroup*.

Building the *Contraction Cover-Up* Page *continued*

13. On to the ovals. It's important to type the word pair that correctly corresponds to the contraction in the oval that you placed in the *back* layer of the page. Click on the *Text* tool, then click on that oval. Now type "can not." Group the text and oval as you did in the previous step.

Text

14. In the other oval (the one in the front layer of the page), use the *Text* tool to type any word pair that makes up some other contraction, such as "do not." Group the text and the shape as before.

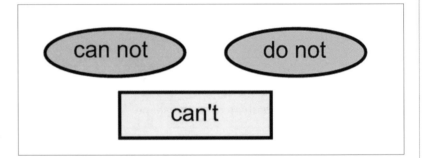

15. Add text in this manner to every set of shapes you have on the page.

16. You're almost finished! The last step is to check your work. Click on a rectangle and drag it up to the oval that contains the correct word pair. The rectangle should cover the oval. Now drag the rectangle over the other oval—the one with the incorrect word pair. This time, the rectangle should disappear.

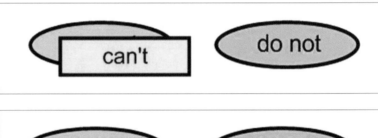

17. If you've gotten everything right, name and save the page. When you are ready, you can add more pages like the one you just made so that your students have plenty of opportunity for practice.

SMART Support for Your Journey

The more you use SMART Notebook software, the more you'll appreciate how versatile and user-friendly it is. But when you're getting started, it can be challenging to remember what each tool in your toolbar can do and how to use all of the software's tools and techniques efficiently and creatively. To help you navigate the learning curve more quickly and easily, I've assembled A Wizard's Guide to SMART Tools and Techniques. This overview, which starts on page 160, is a complete and concise overview of all the tools, tabs, and menu functions I've referred to in Sections 1, 2, and 3 of the book—plus a few extras! Whether you're a beginner or an experienced SMART Notebook user, the Wizard's Guide is a great resource or refresher as questions crop up when you're using the software.

Once you've gotten comfortable with using SMART Notebook software to create engaging lessons in a wide range of content areas, the ultimate stage of your journey is to become Totally SMART by taking advantage of Web-based resources and the online community of SMART Notebook users. So in this section of the book, you'll also find an introduction to the online world of SMART Exchange and other online resources. I've provided my best tips for navigating the SMART Exchange website as well as the names of some of my favorite lessons and how to download and customize them. There will always be something new and cool for your SMART Board, and these resources will help you grow even smarter in the future!

Look here for resources to help you succeed at every stage in your SMART journey.

A Wizard's Guide to SMART Tools and Techniques

The more you use SMART Notebook software, the more you'll appreciate how versatile and user-friendly it is. This overview is designed to help you quickly understand how to access and use the tools, tabs, and menu functions that I've referred to in this book, plus a couple of extras. They're the tools and techniques you'll use most often, but believe me, the software offers many more than I have room to describe here. So once you've mastered these, start exploring the software on your own!

Note that you can access any tool in SMART Notebook either from a computer or from the SMART Board itself. In the explanations below, I talk about "clicking" on tool buttons and options. If you're working directly at your SMART Board, though, you'll be tapping instead of clicking.

SMART Tools

SMART Notebook Software is programmed with a default toolbar that shows tool buttons for the most commonly used tools. Many, but not all, of the tools described below are part of the default toolbar. I recommend customizing (adding buttons to) your toolbar to include all the tools you use on a regular basis. See page 18 for step-by-step instructions on how to access SMART Notebook's big toolbox and add tool buttons to your toolbar lickety-split.

Add Page

Clicking on this tool icon adds a blank page to an open Smart Notebook file. I suggest using this tool when you're in the middle of an activity and want to show your students something new. In essence, the added page is "scrap paper" for you to work on. When you're finished with the activity, if you don't want to save the added page, simply click on *No* in the pop-up window when you close the file.

Clear Ink

"Ink" is anything you add to a page using a *Pen* tool. Clicking on the *Clear Ink* tool instantly erases ink only, leaving the rest of your page intact.

Color

The *Color* tool button usually appears in the toolbar area when you click on the *Pens, Text,* or *Shapes* tool buttons. Clicking on the *Color* button will bring up the color palette, which offers 40 choices of line and/or fill color. (You can also access the color palette through the *Properties* tab.)

Dual Page Display

This tool allows you to display two consecutive pages of a file simultaneously. To find this tool, first click on the *View Screens* tool. *Dual Page Display* will be one of the options in the drop-down menu. When you're in dual-page mode, click on the *View Screens* tool, and you'll see the *Single Page Display* option. Clicking on that option restores your screen to a single-page view. You can customize your toolbar to add the *Dual Page Display* button to it.

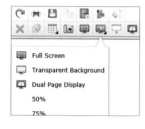

Eraser

On an old-fashioned chalkboard, an eraser will clear away everything. But on a SMART Board, the *Eraser* tool clears "ink" only—markings made with any of the *Pen* tools. Click on the *Eraser* button, and then use your cursor to selectively wipe out ink markings.

"Erasing" Text and Objects

There are a few SMART tricks to try if you want to "erase" a shape, an image, or typed text.

- Select the item you want to get rid of, click on the menu arrow at the corner of the blue frame, and choose *Delete* in the drop-down menu. The item will disappear.

- Add the *Delete* tool to your toolbar. Then you can select an item and click on the *Delete* button.

- Add the *Clear Page* tool to your toolbar, but watch out! When you click on this tool, it will wipe out *everything* on the page: ink, images, shapes, and typed text.

Insert Ruler

As its name suggests, this tool automatically inserts a ruler onto a SMART Notebook page. To make the ruler longer or shorter, click on the far right end of it and drag across your screen to the desired length. You can add this tool button to your toolbar or access it from the *Insert* drop-down menu.

Lines

Add straight or curved lines to a page using this tool. Click on the *Lines* tool button and a menu of additional buttons will appear in your toolbar. Click on the color, line thickness, and line style you wish, then bring your cursor to your page and click and drag until the line is the desired length.

Next Page

Tap this tool button to advance through the pages of a multipage file one at a time. (Tap the adjacent button with the left-pointing arrow on it to move backward page by page.)

Pens

Simply click on this tool button and you can handwrite or draw on your SMART Board using your finger. You can also "draw" with your cursor on your computer screen. SMART Notebook 11 offers a basic pen plus six special types of pens.

To choose the color and thickness of the line. Click on the *Properties* tab or on the color palette in the toolbar. You can also choose to make dotted lines and other line styles.

To choose one of the special pens. Click on the *Pen Types* icon and then select the type of pen you wish from the drop-down menu. (You can also customize your toolbar so that each special pen shows up on its own button.)

Print

This tool is similar to the Print function of most types of computer software, but the tool button for it is not included in the default toolbar. You'll probably want to add it to your toolbar so that you can print any of your SMART Notebook pages from the computer your board is connected to.

Three Special Pens

Creative Pen

Rainbow-hued lines and daisy chains are just two of the possibilities when you draw with the *Creative Pen*. Use this tool for creating fanciful numerals or letters.

To make a pictograph. Simply pop the pen quickly in one spot. Each time you pop it, it will leave one image, such as a smiley face, at that spot.

Highlighter Pen

This pen works just like the old-fashioned kind we used as college students. There are four standard color options and two thickness options, but you can also make other choices from the *Properties* tab or by clicking on the *Color* tool button.

Magic Pen

The *Magic Pen* has three separate features: the spotlight effect, the magnifying effect, and the disappearing ink effect. This pen is designed for use at the SMART Board only: The special effects it creates are temporary and will not save.

To make a spotlight. Click on the *Magic Pen* tool, and then draw a circle or an oval on your page. Be sure to close the shape—this pen can be a little fussy. If you don't succeed the first time, just try again. To move the spotlight around your page, bring your cursor to the edge of the spotlight, and it will change into a hand. Then you can drag the spotlight. To make the spotlight bigger or smaller, bring your cursor to the middle of the spotlight and move it to the left or right or up or down to make the spotlight larger or smaller. (This maneuver takes some practice.) Once you're done with the spotlight, click the x in the upper right corner and the page will be brought back to its original state. You might use this pen feature to bring students' attention to a particular section of a Web page you're viewing on your board.

To make a magnifier. Click on the *Magic Pen* tool and then draw a rectangle (it doesn't have to be perfect, but the shape must be closed). When you get it right, it will transform to a magnifier rectangle, which you can move, resize, or get rid of just as you would a spotlight. This option might be used to bring a section of a picture forward for closer examination and description.

To write in disappearing ink. Open lines, shapes, and letters drawn with the *Magic Pen* begin to fade out after a few seconds. If you're writing letters or numbers, take care not to close shapes (such as the number zero), or you may end up with a spotlight! Writing with fading ink is a fun way to review math facts. Write an expression on the SMART Board and challenge your students to write the answer on individual whiteboards before the disappearing ink fades completely.

Regular
Polygons

Regular Polygons

Click or tap on this tool, and a selection of different polygon buttons will appear in your toolbar area, along with the *Color, Line Style,* and *Transparency* buttons. Click on the polygon you want, then click on your page and drag your cursor until the shape is the desired size. See also *Shapes* on page 166; the instructions for working with shapes also apply to polygons.

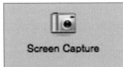

Screen Capture

Area Capture

Screen Capture

Isolate and save elements of a SMART Notebook page, a Web page, digital images, portions of a Word document, and more, using this tool. The elements you capture will be copied and placed on a new page in whatever SMART Notebook file you have open on your computer. This tool operates four different ways, and those four options are illustrated in the special *Screen Capture* toolbar that pops up on your screen when you click on the *Screen Capture* button in your main toolbar. I have given each function a descriptive name to help you remember what it does. (A note for Mac users: The positions of the buttons in your *Screen Capture* toolbar may be different from what is shown here.) Notice too that the toolbar includes a *Capture to new page* check box. If you uncheck the box, the elements you capture will be captured to the actual SMART Notebook page you have open at that moment.

Click and Drag Capture. When you click on this toolbar button (which is also called *Area Capture),* your cursor turns to crosshairs. Move the cursor close to the object(s) you want to capture and click and drag a rectangle around the objects. Once you've framed all the elements you want, release your mouse. Those objects will automatically be captured and appear on a new page in your Smart Notebook file. This is useful when making a collage, creating a presentation, or anytime you want to customize the image you're using instead of using the entire thing.

Clump Capture

Clump Capture. Use this option to capture portions of your screen in clumps that are determined by the software. Click on the *Clump Capture* button (also called *Window Capture),* and your cursor will turn to a circle with crosshairs. Gray or black diagonal lines will appear on a portion of your screen, depending on where you position the cursor. When the lines appear over the portion of the screen you want to capture, click and release your mouse. That portion of the screen will be copied onto a new page in the file. You cannot influence how the software chooses to apportion parts of the screen. I use this option when I want to capture a large section of a page (but not the whole page).

Full Screen Capture

Screen Capture. Use this option (also called *Full Screen Capture*) when you want to capture a copy of your entire screen and place it on a new page in the file.

Freehand Capture

Freehand Capture. Click on this button and then trace freehand around the part of the screen you want to capture. For example, you may want to capture just the eyes from the image of an iguana you found on a Web page. The captured part of the image will be placed automatically on a new page in whatever Smart Notebook file you have open on your computer.

Screen Shade

Screen Shade

Click on the *Screen Shade* tool to place a gray screen over an entire page. The screen can be pulled back to reveal the content underneath by clicking and dragging on the dimple on the gray screen. To remove a screen shade from a page, simply click on the *Screen Shade* tool again.

Select

Select

Think of the *Select* tool as a way of getting into neutral: Clicking on the *Select* button deactivates any other tool, such as *Shapes* or *Lines*. After clicking on the *Select* tool, click on a particular item, image, or text on your screen to select just that object. A blue frame will appear around the object, and that frame offers several possibilities for interacting with that object.

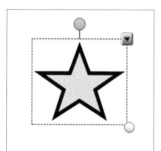

To move an object. Position your cursor anywhere inside the frame and it will turn to a four-headed arrow. Click and drag to move the selected object anywhere on the page, then simply release your mouse.

To rotate an object. Notice the green rotation handle at the top of the frame. Click on it and drag your mouse clockwise or counterclockwise to rotate the object to any angle you choose.

To resize an object. Notice the gray circle at the lower right corner of the frame (the circle is called the resize button or resize handle). Click on that button and drag your mouse in or out to make the object bigger or smaller.

Shapes

Fill a page with circles, rectangles, ovals, and more using the *Shapes* tool. When you click on this tool, a menu of shapes will appear in the toolbar area. To the right of the shape option icons, you may see a small black menu arrow. Click on that, and additional shape options will appear. Click on the shape of your choice, then move your cursor to the screen and click and drag across the screen. Release when the shape is the size you wish. You can add color or texture to shapes before or after adding them to a page by working with the *Color* tool or through the *Properties* tab.

Table

Use this tool to insert a blank table onto a page. When you click on this tool, an 8 x 8 array will appear. Move your cursor across the array to shade the number of rows and columns you want your table to display. Then click your mouse and a table with those dimensions will appear on the page.

To move the table. Click on the gray box in the upper left corner of the table, then drag and drop it. (If the gray box is not there, click and drag across the entire table to make it appear.)

To make the entire table larger or smaller. Click on the resize button at the lower right corner and drag in or out.

To adjust individual column width and row height. Position your cursor on one of the table's dividing lines; your cursor will change to a two-headed arrow. Click and drag the line up or down or side to side.

To add text to a cell. Double-click on the cell and then type.

To fill a cell with color. Double-click on the cell and then open the color palette by clicking on the *Color* button or the *Properties* tab and select the color you wish. If you want to fill the entire table with color, select the entire table and then open the palette and choose your color.

Text

This tool allows you to place typed text anywhere on a page. Click on the *Text* tool icon, and then click anywhere on the white space of the page. A text box will appear. Text options will also appear in the toolbar (and in the *Properties* tab if it's open.) The choices should look familiar—similar to those in the word processing program you use. Either before you begin typing or after you finish, you can change the font, font size and color, and the justification of the text. Boldface, underlining, and italicizing are available too.

You can add as many text boxes to a page as you wish, and each one can be different in font and style if desired. If you need to change some text, because it is misspelled, for example, just double-click on the text and the editing options for font, font color and size, and so on will reappear in the toolbar.

Transparency

The *Transparency* tool button usually appears in the toolbar area when you click on the *Pens, Text, Lines,* or *Shapes* tool buttons. Use this tool to make an object, image, or text have a see-through quality. When you click on this tool button, a sliding tab will pop up on the screen. Use your cursor to slide the tab to achieve the desired transparency of the item you've selected.

SMART Tabs

The tabs in SMART Notebook software are found along the left- or right-hand edge of the screen. Each tab displays an icon. Clicking on a tab icon opens that tab in the sidebar column. Using tabs is a quick way to access some important and highly useful features of the software. *Page Sorter, Gallery,* and *Properties* are the three tabs I use all the time. Here's what they can do for you.

Page Sorter Tab

Click on this tab to view thumbnails of all the pages in the file you have open. If you want to change the order of pages, simply click on the thumbnail of a page and drop and drag it to its new location. Each thumbnail in the *Page Sorter* tab also has its own drop-down menu. To access it, click on the thumbnail and a menu arrow will appear. Click on the menu arrow, and here are some of your options:

Reset Page. Choosing this will restore the page to its last saved state.

Clone Page. Choosing this adds an exact replica of the page in the next slot.

Add Page to Gallery. Choosing this will add the page to a special collection of your "stuff" called *My Content*, which you can access from the *Gallery* tab. With this feature you can insert pages that you've created into other SMART Notebook files. After all, you may invest considerable time in making a page from scratch, so use your creativity to figure out how to adjust the content of your pages for use in another subject area.

Gallery Tab

The *Gallery* is an awesome collection of pictures, programmable interactive templates, and hundreds of other objects you can insert in SMART Notebook files. You'll also find that special collection of your stuff called *My Content*. Click on the *Gallery* tab and a directory will appear that starts with *My Content, Gallery Essentials,* and *Lesson Activity Toolkit* folders. Below the directory is a listing of categories for the selected folder, such as *Pictures, Interactive and Multimedia,* and *Notebook Pages and Files*. Click on one of these to open thumbnails of the contents of that category. You can import any of these pictures, templates, pages, and other items into an open SMART Notebook file simply by double-clicking on the thumbnail or clicking on it and dragging and dropping it. Typing keywords such as "American history" or "mammals" in the search box at the top of the tab will help you locate pictures, objects, and files related to particular topics.

Gallery Essentials. This part of the *Gallery* contains thousands of pictures, photos, and maps and hundreds of interactive objects you can use as is or customize to meet your needs. Once you've added a *Gallery* image or object to a page, you can select it and move it, resize it, or clone it, just as you would a shape or text. Some of the objects have sounds or actions attached to them.

Lesson Activity Toolkit. Look here for interactive templates, among other things, that you can customize to reflect the content you wish.

Properties Tab

Click here to access options such as changing the colors of lines and shapes, changing text style and size, and changing the transparency of objects and images. The options available to you will depend on what kinds of items are on the page and which tool you've selected. I like to use the *Fill* effects option. Choices include filling with a color gradient (which goes from dark to light) or a variety of lined patterns—check it out!

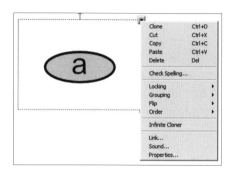

SMART Menu Functions

To access these menu functions, first select an object, image, text, or other element on your screen that you want to manipulate. Then click on the gray menu arrow at the upper right corner of the frame around the selected element, and a drop-down menu with a list of choices will appear.

Clone

Choose the *Clone* feature when you want to make a duplicate of an element on your screen. The cloned object, image, or text can be treated like any other object on the page.

Flip

Flip an object upside down or right side up, or flop it left or right. You will usually use this option with pictures, shapes, or photos.

Grouping

Grouping objects allows you to move, resize, or otherwise manipulate them as a single unit. To group items, click and drag your cursor across all of the objects you want to include until a frame appears around each one. Click on the gray menu arrow of one of those frames and choose *Grouping* and then *Group*. The software now reads those objects as one. If you ever want to ungroup them, right-click on one of the objects and choose *Grouping* and then *Ungroup*.

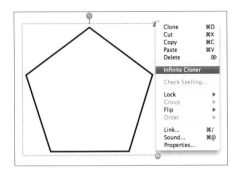

Infinite Cloner

This feature allows you to make as many copies of a selected object as you wish. Click on the gray menu arrow and choose *Infinite Cloner*. Then click and drag repeatedly to make copies. Keep in mind that you must click on the original object to make a copy—not on one of the clones. You'll know which item is the original because when you click on it you'll see a sideways figure 8 (the universal symbol for infinity) in place of the menu arrow on the frame. To turn off the *Infinite Cloner* function, right-click on the object and uncheck the check box.

Link

You can link an object on a SMART Notebook page to a Web page, to another document or a video stored on your hard drive, and to other pages in the same SMART Notebook file. Select the object, click on the menu arrow, and choose *Link* in the drop-down menu. A pop-up window will appear.

To link to a Web page. Copy and paste the Web page address in the *Address* box. (Take care to copy and paste precisely the address for the particular page you want to link to.) Then click *OK*. Now when you tap or click on that object on the SMART Notebook page, it will immediately open the linked Web page. This function is great for science and social studies lessons.

To link to a file on your computer. Click on that option in the pop-up window and then click on *Browse* to search for the file. Click on the file name and then *OK*.

To link to another SMART Notebook page. Click on that option in the pop-up window and then on the desired page in the list of pages. Then click *OK*.

When you've traveled to the linked page and want to return to the original SMART Notebook page, tap on the icon for the file at the bottom of the screen.

Locking

To lock an element in place on a page, select it, open the drop-down menu, and choose *Locking* and then *Lock In Place*. This makes the element unmovable and unchangeable (for example, you can't change its size or color). Locked items show a small padlock icon instead of a menu arrow when they are selected. If you want to unlock an object, click on that padlock and choose *Unlock*.

Order

Smart Notebook pages have four layers. You can move individual items into different layers of a page, which allows them to be superimposed on one another. For example, you might want a shape to cover up a word so that you can then reveal it during an activity. To move a selected object into a different layer in the page, choose *Order* in the drop-down menu and then one of the four options. *Bring to Front* and *Send to Back* are the ones you will use most often. If you want something to be hidden by another object, for example, choose *Send to Back*, which will move the object to the last of the four layers. *Send Backward*, in contrast, moves an item back by just one layer from its current position.

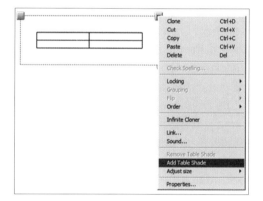

Table Shade

This feature is for tables only. When you select a table and choose the *Add Table Shade* option, each cell of the table will be covered with an individual screen or shade. To reveal what's beneath the shade, tap or click on the dimple that appears in the middle of the shade. To replace the shade on any cell, tap or click the small gray triangle in the upper left corner of the cell. If you ever want to remove a table shade completely, select the table, open the drop-down menu, and choose *Remove Table Shade*.

SMART Exchange: exchange.smarttech.com

By far the largest depository online for SMART Board lessons and activities is SMART Exchange™. It's an area of the SMART Technologies website where teachers can upload lessons they've created and are willing to let others use, search for lessons specific to their grade level and subject area, and locate resources that correlate to specific state or Common Core State Standards.

This site is like a potluck supper. There's a wide variety to choose from, provided by a host of different users. Teachers from all over the globe bring their dishes to share. And like a pot-luck supper, some choices are likely to be tastier (more fun) than others, and some will be highly nutritious (educational). Some might be a week's worth of meals (multipage lessons), while others will be a midnight snack (short and sweet). There might even be a few junk food items that don't quite satisfy your hunger (a sparse one-page activity).

One of my favorite aspects of SMART Exchange is that the content is teacher-sustained—and that means it's ever-changing. Because users add content literally every day, you'll likely find new and interesting lesson ideas every time you visit.

SMART Search Strategies

SMART Exchange is a wonderful resource for all things SMART, but with that wonderfulness come a lot of features to navigate. It can be time-consuming—I know, I've spent a lot of time there! Here are my best tips and suggestions for searching the site efficiently.

The Search Page

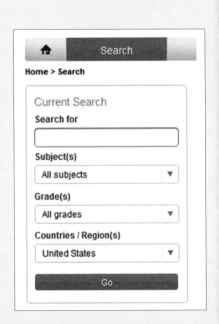

One popular way to search SMART Exchange is to use the Search page features. On the home page, first click on the *Search* tab at the top of the page. This will open the Search page. You can type a key-word in the *Search for* box at top left and narrow your search using the drop-down menus for subject and grade level. Keyword choices can be a lesson topic, such as Geometry or Synonyms. But don't limit yourself to general terms like that. You'd be amazed at the range of lessons on SMART Exchange. Try searching for the name of a book you plan to use with your students, such as *Mrs. Wishy-Washy,* or a holiday you'll be studying, such as Martin Luther King Day.

Narrowing Your Search

No matter what keyword you search for, chances are your search results may seem overwhelming, delivering hundreds of possible choices. You'll need some help narrowing the field. Use the *Narrow Results* box, which sorts your current results by SMART product and program labels, such as SMART Notebook dual-user lessons, SMART Response™ question sets, or SMART Table™ activity packs. Usually, the first category listed is SMART Notebook lessons, and that's what you want. Click on that to remove the other types of products from your results.

> Narrow Results
>
> ▶ **All Types** (50,105)
>
> SMART Notebook lessons (19,165)
>
> SMART Notebook dual user lessons (59)
>
> SMART Notebook Math Tools lessons (410)
>
> SMART Response questions (11,482)
>
> SMART Response question sets (1,368)
>
> SMART Table activity packs (1,526)
>
> SMART Table applications (16)
>
> 3D content (139)
>
> Gallery Collections (340)
>
> Manipulatives (497)
>
> Images (14,781)
>
> PDFs (108)
>
> SMART Sync Collaborations (12)
>
> SMART Ideas (37)
>
> Videos (137)
>
> Widgets (28)

Now you'll have a list of thumbnails and descriptions of all the resources uploaded to SMART Exchange that correlate to your search criteria. You can browse this list to your heart's content—or as long as time allows. I like to use the *Click to Preview* button (at the base of each thumbnail) to get a quick glimpse of a lesson. Keep in mind that some lessons are a single page, but many are multipage. When you preview the activity, you will see the number of pages in the upper left corner of the preview screen. If it's multipage you'll probably want to take a peek at what's included. To move through the pages in preview mode, use the arrow on the middle right side of the preview screen.

Whack-A-Mole [SMART Notebook lesson]

A game where students can throw a koosh ball at the moles to open up a question. This game can be customized ...

Subject: Mathematics, Other

Grade: Pre-Kindergarten, Kindergarten, Grade 1, Grade 2, Grade 3, Grade 4, Grade 5, Grade 6, Grade 7, Grade 8, Grade 9, Grade 10, Grade 11, Grade 12

Submitted by: Jaime Donally

Search terms: scatterplot, mean

> Because users add content to SMART Exchange literally every day, you'll likely find new and interesting lesson ideas every time you visit.

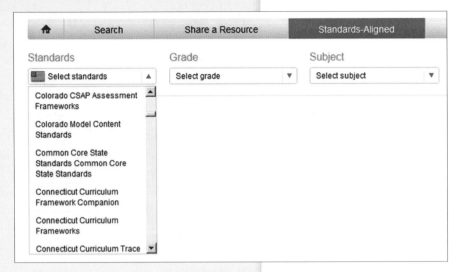

Searching Curriculum Standards

You may want to search for lessons that correlate to state-specific standards or the Common Core State Standards. SMART Exchange is there to help! On the home page, click on the *Standards-Aligned* tab. A page will open with three drop-down menus to help you refine your search: *Standards, Grade,* and *Subject.* In the *Standards* tab, scroll down to find the name of your state, or you can choose the *Common Core State Standards* option. Once you've selected the standard, choose the desired grade level and subject area and click the *View* button.

Downloading from SMART Exchange

When you find an activity you want to use, click the *Download* button next to the thumbnail. In the pop-up window, choose *Save File.* It should save in the Downloads section of your computer's hard drive. Most downloads are free, but there may be a small fee for some.

To access a downloaded file, go to your Documents shortcut on your desktop or the Document section in your Start menu. Click on *Downloads* and locate the file on that list. The file name will be the same as or similar to that used on SMART Exchange (the name of the person who originally submitted the file may be appended to the file name). Once you've found the file in your download list, right-click it and then choose *Send To.* From there you can choose where you want this file to live—your Documents folder is your best bet or, if you have an online storage account with a service such as Dropbox, you can also send it there. Online storage can be a good idea if you work on both your computer at home and a computer at your school. Just a quick note: When you attempt to download something from SMART Exchange for the first time, the site will ask you to register a user name and password. Setting up the account is free and the site doesn't send you loads of email, so you shouldn't feel concerned about doing so.

Working with Downloaded Materials

In most cases, you will be able to alter the contents of files that you download from SMART Exchange. For example, you might find a lesson with a format you love, but the specifics of the content are too advanced for your students. This is often true of review games and templates you might find on SMART Exchange, such as Jeopardy.

The techniques for changing content are the same as those you've learned and practiced in Section 3 of this book. Click on the content you'd like to edit. Check the symbol at the upper right corner of the blue frame: A little padlock means the object is locked. Click on the padlock and choose the *Unlock* option, and you'll be free to edit.

The SMART Community

Another option on the home page of SMART Exchange is a tab titled *Community.* Think of this as SMART social networking—a place where people can post thoughts, ideas, and questions. A variety of forums are inside the *Community* tab, and they will change periodically. The forums cover topics such as SMART products and upcoming SMART events, contests, and grant opportunities. You might even find a user group for your state. You can visit these forums and read what others have added, and you can even write a post yourself if you're feeling smart. Check it out to see whether there is something in the SMART Community for you!

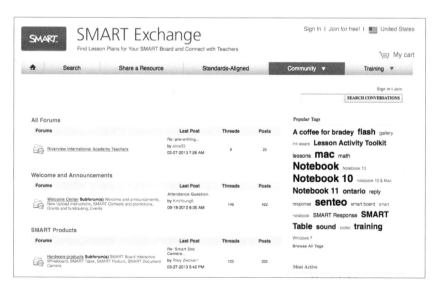

General-Review Game Boards

Download and customize these activities with your own content—these are really great! You can adapt them with content in nearly any subject area, for any grade level. You can search for these general-review game boards by subject area also to see if someone created a game that reviews a concept you've studied. Just use the title provided below to search for them.

- SMART Board Jeopardy

- Connect Four

- Game Board for Review

- Review Bingo

- Koosh Ball Game Template

Some SMART Exchange Favorites

There are thousands of lessons on SMART Exchange; below are a few that I think are particularly well designed and effective and that your students will love. In the chart, you'll see the subject area and grade level I used as keywords when searching the site as well as the title of each game. Also included is the name or alias of the person who submitted the activity, when known. I've included a quick description of each activity to help you determine whether it's worth a peek on your part.

ACTIVITY TITLE	SUBJECT/ GRADE LEVEL	DESCRIPTION
Fact and Opinion	English Language Arts, Grades 2, 3 Submitted by pmack	Each page offers multiple opportunities to teach the skill and some helpful tips on discerning facts and opinions. Some of the pages link the user to fact and opinion games on sites such as PBS Kids. Utilizes many of the interactive templates available in SMART Notebook software.
Synonyms and Antonyms Notebook	English Language Arts, Grades 2, 3, 4 Submitted by lissarodgers	A nice variety of pages: some interactive, some informative, and some that link you to games that allow for the application of the skill.
Math Fact Families	Mathematics, Grades 1, 2, 3 Submitted by Unknown	A varied approach to making fact families. Students make fact families based on three given numbers placed on an image of a house's roof; students use a set of manipulatives to decide what numbers belong in the fact family; students work with numbers but in a fact triangle or number-bond format.
Fractions	Mathematics, Grades 1, 2, 3 Submitted by lissarodgers	Fractions are tricky, and this SMART lesson does a nice job of explaining and labeling them with words and images. Once the use of fractions has been explained, students are given an opportunity to apply what they learned with a variety of tasks. A nice setup! There are links to two fraction games on the last page, which is always a good culminating piece.
How to Read a Map	Social Studies, Grades 1, 2, 3 Submitted by BArnett	The visuals here are appealing, and there is just the right amount of information on the explanatory pages, each with an interactive component. This activity not only teaches basics like the use of a compass rose but also delves into map keys, and it gives students chances to practice everything.
George Washington / Abe Lincoln Comparisons	Social Studies, Grades 1, 2, 3 Submitted by Unknown	Presidents are always a popular social studies topic, and this activity instills a nice blend of activities to reach its goal. There are fill-in-the-blank pages, word sorts, drag-and-drop Venn diagrams, and a culminating image sort to top it all off.
Solar System	Science, Grades 1, 2, 3, 4, 5 Submitted by Unknown	Unique images with labels and opportunities for students to answer questions using the diagrams as guides—a great tie-in to Common Core State Standards! Includes sorting pages of all sorts and a comparison of Earth and Mars at the end that uses a cool technique.
Ecosystem Food Chain and Food Web	Science, Grades 3, 4, 5 Submitted by reneefruge	Offering a picture sort of living and nonliving things, information on the kinds of consumers one finds in a variety of ecosystems, interesting visuals to translate the food chain, and plenty of opportunities for students to create food chains and webs with *Gallery* images, this activity is really well done. Also includes links to some food-chain games (who knew?!) and a Q & A section at the end with links back to the pages that contain the answers. Very clever!

More Online Options

While you could explore the SMART Exchange website forever, you may also want to take a side trip to one of these sites too. Their offerings are a bit different in both style and substance.

PBS Kids: pbskids.org/whiteboard

Most educators love and trust public television, so it's very exciting that PBS has gotten in on the interactive whiteboard action! Each of the interactive games on this site is hosted by a PBS character such as Curious George or Arthur. The games cover language arts, math, and social sciences and span grade ranges from kindergarten through fifth grade. Topics range from civics, natural sciences, and vocabulary to measurement, numbers and operations, reading comprehension, and emergent literacy skills.

Navigation Tips for PBS Kids

It's easy to make your way around this site. The link above will take you directly to the interactive whiteboard games page. From there you can click on the subject area you want and view a chart that displays the name of the game, a description, the grade level(s) it targets, topics covered, and whether audio is needed to play the game.

Click on the game you want to play (note that you'll need to be Internet connected to run these games from the PBS site). Some of the games are housed right on the PBS Kids site and will start to load immediately. However, the games can take a few moments to load, so it's a good idea to start the download before you ask your students to gather in front of the board.

For some games, a pop-up window will appear stating: "You are leaving PBS Kids." Click on the link that says: "Continue to (game name)." This, oddly enough, kicks you into SMART Exchange, where you can download and save the game as described previously in the navigation tips for SMART Exchange.

Scholastic: scholastic.com/teachers

Scholastic is a long-lived resource for educators, and it also offers some interactive whiteboard options on its website. When you go to the site listed above, look for the blue bar near the top of the page. Find the *Student Activities* tab and hover your cursor over it. In the drop-down menu, click on *Interactive Whiteboard Activities*. This page has tabs for Language Arts, Science and Math, Social Studies, and Learning Games and Teaching Tools. Many of these games have an audio component, and they touch on everything from phonics and Black history to weather and word problems.

Occasionally, Scholastic creates holiday or theme-specific interactive activities that are available for use for a limited time. I like to check the site at the beginning of each month to see whether anything special is coming up.

References

Ball, B. 2003. "Teaching and learning mathematics with an interactive whiteboard." *Micromaths* 19 (1): 4–7.

Beauchamp, G., and J. Parkinson. 2005. "Beyond the 'wow' factor: developing interactivity with the interactive whiteboard." *School Science Review* 86 (316): 97–103.

Betcher, C., and M. Lee. 2009. *The Interactive Whiteboard Revolution: Teaching with IWBs*. Victoria, Australia: ACER Press.

Brown, S. 2003. "Interactive whiteboards in education." Joint Information Systems Committee Technology Centre. http://www.jisc.ac.uk/uploaded_documents/Interactivewhiteboards.pdf.

Johnson, D. 2012. *The Classroom Teacher's Technology Survival Guide*. San Francisco: Jossey-Bass.

Marzano, R. J., and M. Haystead. 2009. *Final Report on the Evaluation of the Promethean Technology*. Englewood, CO: Marzano Research Laboratory.

November, A. 2010. *Empowering Students with Technology*. Thousand Oaks, CA: Corwin Press.

Riddle, J. 2009. *Engaging the Eye Generation: Visual Literacy Strategies for the K–5 Classroom*. Portland, ME: Stenhouse.

Sprenger, M. 2010. *Brain-Based Teaching in the Digital Age*. Alexandria, VA: ASCD.

Index

Also Available from Crystal Springs Books

Accidental Techie to the Rescue!
Simple Tech Solutions for Your Biggest Classroom Challenges

LORI ELLIOTT, EDD, "THE ACCIDENTAL TECHIE"

"Accidental Techie" and former teacher Lori Elliott has researched loads of great websites so you don't have to. You'll learn how to use technology to engage students, build collaboration skills, interact with classrooms around the globe, and more. With Lori as your guide and technology as a tool, you and your students will reach new heights of enthusiasm and learning.

(K–6) 224 pp. #550227

Teach Like a Techie *20 Tools for Reaching the Digital Generation*

LORI ELLIOTT, EDD, "THE ACCIDENTAL TECHIE"

You can meet the digital natives on their own turf with this step-by-step guide to educational technology. Podcasts? Prezi? Google Earth? Blogs? No problem, with the "Accidental Techie" as your guide. Lori focuses not on bells and whistles but on simple applications that can immediately bring new relevance, energy, and enthusiasm to your classroom.

(K–12) 192 pp. #550209

Engineer Through the Year, Grades K–2
20 Turnkey STEM Projects to Intrigue, Inspire & Challenge

SANDI REYES

Present your class with the exciting challenges in this book, all built to fold right into your current curriculum. Introduce students to Sandi's simple five-step engineering design process. Then, as you guide them with careful, consistent questioning, watch your budding engineers apply their knowledge to design their own unique drums and sailboats, kites and umbrellas, fish catchers, mailboxes, and so much more.

(K–2) 176 pp. #550237

Interventions for All: Phonological Awareness

YVETTE ZGONC

This jam-packed volume, incorporating some of the elements that made Yvette's *Sounds in Action* so popular, is just what you need to build phonological awareness. Identify strengths and weaknesses through a simple, reproducible assessment and then turn to the brand-new interventions to match student needs. Includes a Spanish version of the assessment (perfect for ELL), activities for all tiers of RTI, a study guide, and more!

(K–2) 176 pp. #402680

Math Talk *Teaching Concepts & Skills Through Illustrations & Stories*

CHAR FORSTEN & TORRI RICHARDS

Using fanciful illustrations of nursery rhymes and thematic scenes, you will be able to: engage your students in fun but focused discussions, inspire them to create and share their own math stories, establish home-school connections so children can "talk math" with parents and siblings, differentiate instruction, and scaffold content for diverse learners.

(PreK–1) 80 pp. #402657